Becoming
a Psychologist
in Australia

Marion Kostanski

AUSTRALIAN ACADEMIC PRESS
Brisbane

First published in 2006 by
Australian Academic Press
32 Jeays Street
Bowen Hills Qld 4006
Australia
www.australianacademicpress.com.au

National Library of Australia
Cataloguing-in-Publication data:

> Kostanski, Marion, 1955– .
> Becoming a psychologist in Australia.
>
> ISBN 1 875378 73 1.
>
> 11. Psychologists - Training of - Australia. I. Title.
>
> 150.23

Cover and text designed by Andrea Rinarelli of Australian Academic Press.

Contents

About the
author

Marion is currently employed as a Senior Lecturer at Victoria University, Melbourne. She studied for her undergraduate degree as a mature-age student, and progressed from there to complete a Graduate Diploma in women's studies, a Bachelor of Education in counselling, a Master of Psychology (child and education) and a PhD, writing a thesis on the 'Genesis of Body Image Dissatisfaction in Children'. During this period of her life she worked part-time as a tutor, research assistant, counsellor and private practitioner. Her specialised area of research and practice as a psychologist is working with young people and adolescents in relation to identity development, with a particular interest in eating behaviours and body image issues.

Marion entered the arena of academia in 1995, and has spent many hours teaching, researching with, supervising and mentoring students who have chosen to attend university and study psychology. She is a registered psychologist in the state of Victoria and a full member of the Australian Psychological Society. She is also strongly involved in her community, and has served for three years as the President of the Eating Disorders Foundation of Victoria and two years as President of the Zonta Club of Melbourne CBD, and has held the portfolio of Communication with the Victorian State Branch of the Australian Psychological Society for the past two years.

To contact Marion about this book send her an e-mail with the subject BAP at Marion.Kostanski@vu.edu.au

Introduction

As a field of study, psychology has grown rapidly over the past 15 years. From an obscure area of philosophical discourse to a complete field of professional endeavour, the interest and demand for courses and professional development in the field of psychology has flourished. However, while the profession itself has evolved, the path to obtaining this credential remains somewhat confusing and convoluted for many.

Some of this confusion is due to how the word 'psychology' is used. Psychology is not just a professional label applied to specialists who work within a particular framework; it is also the term applied to a stream of intellectual knowledge. Many people can study psychology as a part of their undergraduate studies for a variety of professions; examples include degrees in teaching, business management, nursing, research, alternative medicine, science, biochemistry, hospitality, journalism, community development, welfare, social work and human resource management. Students in these courses have an interest in psychology as a discipline and in how psychology can help them perform better in their chosen profession. They believe that the underpinning ideals and approaches of the discipline of psychology can contribute to, and enhance their way of, thinking and working.

Others enter the field of psychological study because they want to work as a psychologist. These people have decided that the discipline and philosophy of psychology will provide them with a rewarding future career.

This book aims to provide some guidance to the student who is not quite sure what they want to achieve and where they eventually want to settle in their career. It provides an overview of the various pathways that can be taken to become a professional psychologist. It also explores some of the more puzzling aspects and theoretical bases within the study of psychology itself. In developing this book I have drawn upon the many hours of consultation I have had with prospective students. While not all the content will be relevant to everyone, there are sections that may be beneficial and may provide some level of clarity when you are making decisions about where you want to focus and diversify your studies. Importantly, it offers assistance to new students wanting to determine their area of specialisation.

I trust the following information will be helpful. I accept that no one publication can ever be all encompassing, particularly in such a complex area. However, following 10 years of teaching, training and supervising students as they negotiate their careers and study choices, I trust I have addressed most of the common concerns we all experience.

If you feel that there are still unanswered questions lurking in the background, please do not hesitate to let me know. I will endeavour to find the answer for you. If there is something you wish to know more about, or if you have additional information to share, please feel free to contact me.

I trust this book does provide you with some assistance and relief. Enjoy your studies.

Cheers,
Marion

What is psychology?

Psychology as a field of study had its foundations in the areas of philosophy, physiology, anatomy, medicine and anthropology. For centuries man has had a strong fascination with trying to unravel the meaning of life. The quest to understand the nature and purpose of man has been the foundation for much of the intellectual and spiritual development of human beings across the ages. However, the full exploration of the human psyche and the importance of the functioning of the human mind did not gain much attention until the beginning of the 19th century.

It was then that a young medical student, Sigmund Freud, developed a method of treating hysterical patients through the use of hypnosis. This was the beginning of psychology as a field of professional activity. It was also the period when Darwin (1809–1882) introduced his famous thesis *The Descent of Man* (1871), and both these men contributed to the exponential growth in what is now known as psychology as a discipline.

Where did psychology come from?

Psychology as a discipline did not truly get established until the mid 19th century. Before then, understandings about human nature were heavily based on knowledge from philosophy, anatomy, physiology, biology and medicine. During this period, physiological science was making strong headway into understanding certain aspects of human behaviour. More particularly, people such as Flourens (1794–1867), Broca (1824–1880), Wernicke (1848–1904) and Muller (1850–1934) had begun to unravel certain mysteries surrounding the importance and functioning of the brain. We first began to learn of the importance of certain bodily functions, and in particular the central importance of the brain in everyday maintenance of life activity. It was these pioneers who identified that specific components and areas of the brain were important for varying functions of the human body, such as speech, movement and sensation. If you want to read more about the impact of this knowledge on human development I suggest you read Stephen Jay's *The Mismeasure of Man* (details in the back of this book).

Simultaneously, biologists were developing their own theories about who man was, and it was Charles Darwin who introduced some definitive answers with his notion of evolutionary science. His research led him to propose that man was a descendant of the apes. Darwin argued that life was a series of evolutionary processes where species learnt to adapt and genetically modify their structure to suit their environment. At the time, many considered Darwin to be a heretic as his research conflicted with the spiritual and central importance of man as a super being, yet recent anthropological works indicate that his theory was soundly based.

Darwin also became known for his scientific exploration of the concept of human emotion and was instrumental in developing what is now known as 'psychometric substantiation'. He introduced a method of systematically collecting data, utilising multiple sources and relying on replicability of his findings — nowadays we call these concepts validity and reliability.

In the late 19th century, Wilhem Wundt (1832–1920) drew heavily on these areas of growing knowledge and introduced the beginnings of a new academic discipline. It was the beginning of the evolution of psychology as a science. Although today much of Wundt's work can be strongly criticised for its lack of scientific rigour, he made a strong contribution to the evolution of scientific psychology through his work examining feeling states and conscious thought processes. Wundt's work was complemented by other researchers such as Gustav Fechner (1801–1887), Herman Ebbinghaus (1850–1909), Georg Muller (1850–1934) and Francis Galton (1822–1911).

Measuring intelligence

It was people such as Galton who moved the study of psychology into the realm of personality, by gathering extensive data sets on individuals and abilities. Karl Pearson (1857–1936), whose particular interest lay in developing an understanding of the average person, further enhanced this work. This type of focus led to our current emphasis on empirical research. The era of statistical analysis and mathematics entered the domain of psychology and Spearman (1863–1945) was at the forefront of this new direction. He became fascinated with the study of the whole person within their natural surroundings and explored how various behaviours were connected. The primary question being explored was that of intelligence.

A key factor being examined was the attempt to uncover whether there was one specific general form of ability, called intelligence, common to all humans. It was Cattell (1905–1998) who advanced Spearman's work and coined the phrase 'mental testing', and began the Society for Multivariate Experimental Psychology. Researchers such as Binet (1857–1911) and Terman (1877–1956) further developed Spearman's work.

Assessment of the human psyche was now established. Intelligence testing and personality assessment were introduced as standard criteria for school selection purposes and was used extensively in World War I by the US Army. One of the ironies of this type of work is that it has led many people to believe that aspects of human functioning are concrete, quantifiable objects. However, it is important to always remember that many of the factors or variables identified in psychology (such as IQ, emotions, memory, etc.) are based on a concept. That means a name has been applied to a factor that has been identified across or within a population of human beings — this has then been assessed deductively and statistical norms applied. What we have is a broad range of identified factors, which are relative only. For example, one cannot be three times as happy, sad or lonely than someone else; they can only be identified as presenting with a level of sadness in relation to a defined measure of this construct. Similarly, one's intelligence quotient (i.e., IQ) is a measure of intelligence, calculated from a series of aptitude tests concentrating on specific verbal and spatial abilities. (An IQ score of 100 represents 'average' intelligence.) It is not a concrete object that can be measured, but it gives psychologists and/or educators an understanding of the level of mastery of identified skills that an individual has in relation to their peer group.

Investigating human behaviour

At the same time that experimental psychology was developing, in the USA an alternative school of psychological knowledge known as Behaviorism was evolving. Whereas the Europeans remained focused on exploring consciousness and higher aspects of mental functioning, the American school was developing their own parameters, primarily based in biological science. For this school, the foundation of psychological science rested in the understanding and explanation of overt human behaviour (what can be seen). One of the founding fathers of this branch of psychology was John Watson (1878–1958). For Watson, the psychology of man was embedded in the study of objectivity. He argued that psychology was a branch of the natural sciences, and was fundamentally about investigating human behaviour. Building on concurrent work by Pavlov (1849–1936), Watson became dedicated to explaining human behaviour in terms of conditioned reflexes. His work was to be further complemented by others, such as Thorndike (1847–1949) and Skinner (1904–1990). These researchers' work set the scene for an ongoing area of psychological research and practice — the notion of learned behaviour and conditioned response.

Cognitive psychology

One further development of the discipline of psychology that was to make a strong mark on our understanding of the human mind and behaviour was that of cognitive psychology. An extension of the behavioural school, cognitivism — through the work of people such as Karl Lashley (1890–1951) — exposed the fundamental limitations of simple reflexology and stimulus recall. These researchers discovered that there were aspects of the brain's functioning wherein it acted like a central storage and retrieval system. They argued that this system was central to our understanding of how the human mind and body functioned as an integrated whole. We learnt about memory and the difference between short-term and long-term processing of information.

Cognitive psychology was adopted and expanded by people such as Piaget (1896–1980) and Kohlberg (1927–1987). It was Piaget who first examined the processes involved in knowledge acquisition. His work uncovered the progressive nature of knowledge and behavioural development, commencing in infancy and progressing through to late childhood. His work helped us understand the processes of development and the sequential nature of learning. Kohlberg further contributed to this work through his research into understanding the nature of empathy and moral development.

The foundations were laid for what is currently known as the discipline of psychology. More recent developments in technology, and importantly the ability to access detailed information through electronic microscopy and computer technology, has meant that the discipline has advanced rapidly since the early 1960s. Currently, research in the area of neurological science and physiology continues to extend and enhance our previous knowledge base.

When I started this explanation of the development of psychology we began with Freud. You may well be asking what happened to the whole issue of a psychologist engaging in psychotherapy, or what has often been called 'the talking cure'? Undeniably, Freud was a very influential person in developing an understanding of the human psyche. He had a strong influence on the whole area of personality development and the introduction of medical science into the equation.

It was the work of people such as Kraeplin (1856–1926), Janet (1859–1947) and Freud (1856–1939) that set the scene for the development of treatment methods within the discipline. Their work was focused on developing a cure for the sick or mentally insane members of society. The central focus of Freud's work was in uncovering the psychic forces that he believed underpinned neurotic behaviour. Most importantly, it was Freud, with the assistance of his mentor and friend Joseph Breuer, who explored the effectiveness of hypnotherapy and catharsis in the treatment of neurotic individuals. Freud's work became extremely popular among a small select group of psychiatrists and medical practitioners within Europe. His ideas were also adopted by others outside the profession and many parallels of his work evolved; however, the underlying principles of psychoanalysis were still considered doubtful. Some followers of the Freudian approach began to diversify and developed their own theories regarding the human psyche and personality. Soon we had Jung (1875–1961), McDougal (1871–1938) and Adler (1870–1937) all proposing variations on the theme of psychoanalysis and many intellectual debates occurred.

The development of psychoanalysis

The main difficulty with psychoanalysis seemed to lay in its 'pseudo-scientific' approach to theoretical development. Many practitioners of this method of treatment despised the popular methods of using quantitative analysis as the basis for scientific rigour. Their work was often based on single case study accounts of illness and a specific approach to treatment. Unfortunately, it was impossible to replicate these treatments; there was no evidence upon which to base any actual claims of cure, and most importantly, two practitioners with differing philosophical backgrounds would often hotly dispute the underpinning components of the same case.

Freudian, Jungian and many other schools of psychoanalysis and psychodynamic interpretations of personality development (i.e., Winedot 1896–1971, Sullivan 1892–1949, Klein 1882–1960) have remained popular as a preferred treatment modality, primarily for psychiatrists, but also many psychotherapists. However, this approach has not been whole-heartedly adopted within psychology as a discipline. More recent developments in research have moved away from the purely scientific approach. The introduction of qualitative methodologies has seen a return to incorporating this alternative therapeutic approach into psychology. This change in direction has been driven by the strongly embedded and ongoing quest for knowledge that has not been addressed by the previous 100 years of research and theoretical knowledge. The questions remain about 'What is it that makes human beings unique'?

Where is the soul and how do we account for all that which is not a sum of the parts? For those interested in this type of academic pursuit or professional development, there are many postgraduate schools of study available. There has been a gradual increase in those pursuing this area of study as schools of psychology begin to incorporate qualitative methods and philosophy back into their curricula.

However, the discipline of psychology as taught within Australian universities remains heavily based on the scientist–practitioner model.

Psychology as a specific profession

Psychology as a profession was formalised in 1892 with the establishment of the American Psychological Association (APA), followed closely by the establishment of the British Psychological Society in 1901. Prior to this, Edward Cox had formally established the Psychological Society of Great Britain, which had functioned for over two decades, and provided the basis for the development of several experimental laboratories. Similarly, some government funding witnessed the short-lived development of laboratories in America and Britain. People such as Galton (1822–1911) and Cattell (1905–1998) established their experimental laboratories and practical connections were made with mental institutions and asylums.

Development of psychology in Britain

The foundation of the British Psychological Society was the obvious outcome of these fledgling organisations. In 1901 its charter identified the aims of the society as 'to advance scientific psychological research, and to further the co-operation of investigators in the various branches of psychology'.

In Britain, the Maudsley Institute of Psychiatry was developed in 1915 and the foundation of the Tavistock Clinic in 1920. An educational branch of the British Psychological Society was also announced in 1919. The discipline of psychology remained a sub-component of study within universities for quite some time and there were few specific departments of psychology until after World War II. In 1948, the Maudsley Institute established its own Department of Psychology.

The British Psychological Society, in 1934, appealed for the formal recognition of psychologists through the establishment of a register. Prerequisites for listing on the register were that the individual show evidence of competence in the theoretical knowledge of psychology and its application to the broader sphere of occupational development, health and education. Moreover, the intending registrant needed to provide evidence of their qualifications, not necessarily through academic study, but more importantly through professional engagement in their work practices. This did not necessarily equate with paid employment, but acknowledged the necessary principle of what would loosely be recognised as apprenticeship.

As with all new institutions, the development of psychology as a profession was not without its conflict. Legally binding criteria and definitions of the profession were not incorporated into the Charter of the Society until 1941. Specialist divisions within the society evolved, with formal recognition of Child Psychology, Clinical Psychology, and Educational Psychology. There was still strong opposition from some quarters to this perceived 'watering' down of the profession. In 1947, in his presidential address to the society, Bartlett claimed that psychology had become too diversified. He maintained that each division was becoming less familiar and there was a tendency to rely on internal jargon and factional splits.

In 1946, a group of five young men formally announced their distrust of the society and criticised it for having neglected the importance of experimental psychology as the basis of the discipline. This was to be the beginning of a separate group, known as the Experimental Psychology Group — known since 1959 as the Experimental Psychological Society.

Development of psychology in North America

Originally, in North America there were the Association of Clinical Psychology, the American Association of Applied Psychology and the APA. There was a strong distinction being made between those who worked as professional practitioners and those who worked in the field of science and psychology as a discipline. The objectives of the APA were defined as advancement of the scientific and professional basis of psychology 'as a means of promoting health, education and human welfare ... thereby to advance scientific interests and inquiry, and the application of research findings to the promotion of health, education and the public welfare'.

Meanwhile in North America, the clinical group rejoined the main body in 1919, but formal recognition of this division within the APA did not occur until 1948. Similarly, the American Association of Applied Psychology rejoined the APA in 1945. It was not until 1948 that specific clinical divisions of Military Psychology, Educational Psychology, Industrial and Business Psychology, Consulting Psychology and Clinical Psychology were recognised. By 1949, in Boulder, Colorado, the APA had defined the scientist–practitioner model of psychology, and the establishment of a PhD as the qualification required for practitioners wanting to undertake clinical psychology.

Since these times the APA has also developed a formal lobby group, identified as the Public Policy Office, which works specifically to liaise with

Capitol Hill (the site of US Congress) and federal agencies to develop legislation, advancement of policy and advocacy of psychology across the nation. The APA now has 55 formal listed divisions of psychological practice, and remains the most influential and powerful organisation for psychologists in the world with over 150,000 members.

Psychology in Australia

Psychologists were first appointed to the Australian government in the early 1920s. At this time, their work was centred on conducting psychological assessments and recruitment for the armed forces, as well as educational institutions. In 1930, The Australian Council for Educational Research (ACER) was founded.

It was not until 1945 that an Australian branch of the British Psychological Society was established.

In 1946, a Department of Psychology was established at Melbourne University. In 1956, the University of Western Australia established a four-year Diploma in Clinical Psychology and, in 1959, the University of Sydney had started a Diploma in Clinical Psychology. By 1960, all established universities in Australia had designated departments of Psychology.

While psychology became established as a recognised discipline within academia, the practice of the profession within the broader community was far more complicated. Indeed, the practice of specific aspects of psychology — particularly education, assessment and counselling — was not considered to be unique to these individuals.

Registration of psychologists as professionals was soon an inevitable necessity if the profession was to be able to claim its rightful place in the area of work and vocation. Although considerable debate occurred, with many dissenting voices, it was recognised that there was a need for a register reflecting the eligibility of persons to practice as psychologists.

Formal recognition of psychology as a profession in Australia did not occur until 1965 when through an Act of Parliament the State of Victoria enacted the *Psychological Practices Act*. The Act was revised in 1973 and further registration of psychologists in Tasmania, South Australia, Western Australia, Queensland and the Northern Territory were soon introduced. *The Psychologists Registration Act 2000* (Victoria) states its purposes to be:

> ... to protect the public by providing for the registration of psychologists and investigations into the professional conduct and fitness to practice as registered psychologists; and to regulate the advertising relating to the provision of psychological practices; and to establish the Psychologists Registration Board of Victoria and the Psychologists Registration Fund; and to repeal the Psychologists Registration Act 1987, and make consequential amendments to other Acts; and to provide for other related matters.

As such, the registration and oversight of psychological practices in Victoria is governed by legislation. Similar Acts exist in other states and territories. The seeming anomaly of the Act being introduced to 'protect the public', as distinct from being to govern or enhance the profession, came about in the 1960s. This was due to the increasing concern of members of the society and parliamentarians in relation to the use of psychological measures — in particular personality tests by religious sects (i.e., Scientologists), other 'cult' groups or individuals to recruit members. Therefore, it was considered righteous and proper that because such measures could not be banned outright, that they be restricted to a limited few who had received 'proper' training and were legally registered to practice.

With the legal recognition of psychology as a profession, the Australian Psychological Society (APS) was also formally incorporated, and became a separate independent body, as distinct from an offshoot of the British Psychological Society.

The aims of the APS are to advance psychology as a discipline and a profession. As a professional association the APS 'strives to promote quality psychological practice, and foster learning and growth, by setting high standards of professional education and conduct'.

In 1968 an Australian code of conduct for psychologists was produced. Finally, in 1972, the APS commenced formal accreditation of all courses of psychology being taught in Australian universities. Heavily based on a scientist–practitioner model, the accreditation of courses involves a strict accreditation process, where schools or departments of psychology are required to submit their curricula for scrutiny and approval by the APS every five years.

Intending psychologists who wish to register as psychologists in Australia are currently required to engage in a formal course of study of no less than four years of an accredited course and a minimum of two years of supervised training. However, the APS currently requires a minimum of six years of formal education and supervision for eligibility as a full member of the society. The student can become confused trying to decipher the differences between these two requirements. Suffice to say that the most important issue for one who wishes to practice as a psychologist is to obtain state registration (i.e., four years plus two). Membership of the APS is an optional choice, similar to deciding whether one desires to formally join a golf club in order to be able to play golf. The benefits of joining a club may not make you a better psychologist, but they can contribute to enhancing your work practices and networks.

Who is a psychologist?

Given the complexity accompanying the development of psychology as a specific discipline and a profession, who then is a psychologist? Among the many options available there are those who adhere to the early ideas of Freud and his followers, and thus engage in the study of psychoanalysis or psychodynamics. Others have maintained a purely scientific and academic approach to exploring psychology as a specific concept of knowledge. Still others have branched out from the area of theory and research into application of these at a practical level. It is these last two groups of people — those who engage in scientific research and theory development or practical application of methods in the population at large — who are known as psychologists.

A psychologist is a person who, having undergone a certain level of recognised formal study and supervised practical work, engages in working with others to better the quality and environmental conditions of life, primarily for other human beings. The APA defines a psychologist as being 'an expert in human behaviour'.

In North America, according to the APA, a professional psychologist is defined as 'having a doctoral degree in psychology from an organised, sequential program in a regionally accredited university or professional school'. Persons with qualifications at a master's degree level are referred to as counsellors, clinicians, or specialists — as distinct from psychologists.

In Britain, however, anyone can call himself or herself a psychologist but, as in Australia, the register of the British Psychological Society provides a listing of those persons who have trained and specialised in psychology as a profession. People can register as a chartered psychologist after achieving the specific required levels of formal qualification and supervised practice.

In Australia, one needs to have completed a minimum of four years formal qualifications through an accredited organisation plus two years of supervised practice. To hold specialist registration it is necessary to have undergone further formal education and supervision.

One other major confounding issue for many people is the distinction between a psychiatrist, psychologist and psychotherapist. Fundamentally, a psychiatrist refers to someone who has completed medical training followed by a specialist study in psychiatry. Psychiatrists generally work with persons who have mental illness, such as bipolar disorder or schizophrenia. Conversely, psychotherapists are persons who have not formally studied either psychiatry or psychology and do not have medical training. The psychotherapist may have studied purely philosophical and/or treatment methods, or combined therapeutic training with formal studies in other disciplines such as social work, occupational therapy, nursing, teaching, and so on. A psychotherapist does not need to have any formal qualifications, nor do many people who call themselves counsellors.

Following the scientist–practitioner model, psychology is a broad term and incorporates a variety of different work practices. It is essential that the budding psychologist first and foremost develops a comprehensive knowledge of the fundamental scientific basis of the discipline, its application to theory and practice, research and assessment processes. Once this level of recognised study has been achieved, the new member of the profession is invited to specialise in their preferred area of discipline knowledge. They will then decide if they want to apply their knowledge and skills within the workplace or enter the academic field of research and teaching. There is often a strong overlap between the two fields, with practitioners engaging in both aspects of the profession.

The psychologist can be found working across a diverse range of areas — such as education, rehabilitation, organisational practices, human resourcing, group dynamics, environmental issues, mental health, and research.

The undergraduate experience

The first step to becoming a psychologist requires completion of an undergraduate psychology major in a formally recognised institution. This is when the specific focus of study is on the underpinning theory and practical basis of the discipline. Often this is a time when students can become frustrated and impatient, especially when they have entered study because they had a general idea of what they wanted to do — often 'to work with, or help people'.

Unlike some other professions, such as social work, occupational therapy, nursing, teaching or welfare studies, the professional development aspect of psychology does not begin until the fourth year of study. The beginning component of the professional program is when the student develops a clear foundation of the discipline itself. It is this foundational structure of study that provides the basis for understanding the discipline and developing a broad understanding of the theoretical and scientific principles that substantiate our work as psychologists.

As shown by the previous discussion, there is no one definite theoretical basis to understanding human behaviour or development. Undergraduate students are invited to explore the historical underpinning of their discipline as they learn about cognitive and emotional development, study neuropsychology and psychopathology. They learn about methods of assessment and evaluation, how to write and to do research, and how to be critical consumers of knowledge. Most importantly, they learn about ethics and the importance of substantiation. There

Table 1

Fundamental steps to attaining a psychologist qualification

1. Undergraduate study
   Accredited 3-year sequence of study taken in conjunction with other
   majors. For students entering higher education for first time.

   1A. Graduate Diploma in Psychological Studies
       For persons who want to return to study psychology having
       previous undergraduate qualifications.

2. Honours, or Graduate Diploma
   Basic requirement for anyone wishing to enter the profession.

3A. Further Study

   Master by Coursework
   A 5th and 6th year of study plus placements, specialisation in field
   of psychology, eligible for registration as a psychologist, eligible
   for membership of APS college.

   DPsych
   Three years of postgraduate study, often an extension of Masters
   program in area of specialisation, eligible for registration, eligible
   for membership of APS college.

   Master or PhD by Research
   Completion of a thesis; extended piece of research, eligible for
   membership of APS, with one-year supervision eligible for registration as a psychologist, basis for employment as an academic.

3B. Supervised practice while formally employed
    Two years of recognised supervision, eligible for registration as a
    psychologist.

4. Ongoing professional development
   Undertaking alternative fields of study, training, research, conference
   attendance and supervision. Open to all members of the profession
   and strongly recommended. Ongoing APS membership requirement.

are eight primary areas of competency required of the undergraduate student — discipline knowledge; research skills; assessment; service implementation; professional, legal and ethical knowledge; communication skills; professional and community networks; and an understanding of agency of change.

It is expected that within an accredited system of undergraduate study the student will have been exposed to a depth of education in the following fields: psychological processes (i.e., cognition, perception, information processing, learning, individual differences, motivation, emotions, etc.); social and biological bases of behaviour; lifespan development; history and theories of psychology; intercultural and indigenous aspects of psychology; psychological testing and assessment; report writing; research design and analysis; and professional ethics.

What your studies will involve

Theories of psychology

From the brief overview provided in chapter one, you will be aware by now that there is no one fixed theoretical basis to the discipline of psychology. Rather, there are multiple levels of inquiry, each one having a specific basis in evolution over the decades as knowledge advanced and technology, economics, philosophy and the sciences have evolved. The student is challenged to begin to unravel all of these differing orientations and develop their own understanding about how these theories are applied to their knowledge of human behaviour, cognitions, emotions and functioning in general.

A theory is defined as 'a coherent group of general propositions used as principles of explanation for a class of phenomena' (*The Macquarie Dictionary*, 1997, p. 2195). Within the discipline you will be exposed to a variety of theoretical viewpoints ranging from behaviourism to humanism and existentialism. The key thing to learn is that there is no one right answer. There are many ways to conceptualise the human being and their place in the world. What is fundamental to psychology is that a theory provides a substantial basis for exploring specific functions and behaviours. It is also the foundation for all research, experimentation and intellectual discourse (communication). A profession needs a sound theoretical basis to its work — whatever you write, think or do in psychology is premised on theory. As individuals you will make choices regarding the most relevant theory for yourself; however, you need to be able to substantiate your position. To do this you need a solid, basic understanding of the varying positions before you decide where your preference lies.

Cognitive–behavioural theory (CBT) is promoted within the scientist–practitioner model of psychology as being the most successful therapeutic approach to understanding and working with human behaviour and psychological problems. This has been based on strong empirical evidence for its application and outcomes that has been established by researchers. However, there are many other therapeutic approaches and treatment modalities that you may prefer. In some instances, CBT may not be the most appropriate treatment to use for specific client/s. There are alternative options (i.e., interpersonal psychotherapy, art therapy, narrative therapy, Gestalt therapy, existentialist therapy, etc.) that are all valid aspects of the discipline and which you may prefer to choose as your central focus.

Cognition

Cognition is the term used to define thinking processes within the human mind and this has been the underpinning of many psychological writings within the past 100 years. Yet there are still many questions that arise in this area; for example: is cognition a tool, an instrument or indeed the absolute? By this do we, as human beings, use the action of thinking to automatically determine our thought processes and knowledge? Is cognition an option to utilise in making decisions and developing our knowledge base? Or is cognition the ultimate aspect of our intrinsic status as human beings?

These are very significant questions, which students will not necessarily encounter until much later in their university studies. During first and second year students will learn about cognitive processes, memory, and the functional aspects of the nervous system and brain that combine to allow us to engage in thoughtful process or thinking.

There are some who argue that thinking is not the absolute, but other intrinsic factors, not as readily observable or quantifiable, drive our fundamental psyche and make humans distinct among species. With recent developments in technology we can now track brain functioning in relation to many aspects of our thought processes, our emotional states. Technology can even help us delve into explaining the tendency of some individuals to have higher levels of spiritual affiliation than others. Just remember that all is not as clear-cut as it seems. Students are able to ponder the rationale behind such a heavy investment in this area of scientific endeavour.

New research indicates that some of the past methods used to support cognitions and behaviour are potentially flawed. Thus, this is an exciting and engaging topic in which to invest one's intellectual energies.

Becoming a Psychologist in Australia

Empiricism

One of the key areas of undergraduate study involves conducting empirically sound research. What do I mean by this? Empiricism is a central tenet of the discipline of psychology. Empirical evidence is something the student will be repeatedly asked for, and this is the foundation upon which the generation of knowledge within psychology as a science is based. To be able to support your views and generate new ideas, hard evidence is required to support assumptions. This is when students will explore empirical databases. These are statistically generated 'facts' related to identifying associations, relationships and predictors of one factor to another. For example, in order to claim that treatment Y is much more effective than treatment P then one needs to provide evidence to support the claim. Similarly, to adopt the philosophical application of one intervention above another to cure anxiety, evidence of this being significant needs to be provided. In psychology, 'significant' means that statistically we find one aspect to be stronger than the other, over and above that which one would find by chance. A heavy focus of your studies in psychology will involve understanding quantitative analysis or statistics.

Despite the emphasis on providing evidence, one cannot ever prove anything by statistical analysis; you are merely looking to support or not support your assumptions.

Research

As you are beginning to realise, an important aspect of all scientifically based knowledge is research. As discussed previously, the foundation of all new knowledge rests on being able to substantiate ideas. Solid evidence needs to be provided to support propositions about how a certain life event or experience occurs or interacts with other factors. Thus the budding psychology student needs to develop a keen understanding of what they are looking for and why. Once you have a hunch, you have explored the literature and decided on a theoretical position, the next thing you need to do is develop a question. When this has been firmly formulated, then the real work begins.

The student learns how, through a process of experimental research, to extend their hypotheses into a developed study of human nature and determine whether or not there is support for their proposition. There are two main methods used for this purpose, the first of which is the area of statistical analysis. Also known as quantitative methods, statistical methodology is considered to be the one and only true basis for scientific knowledge as accepted by mainstream practitioners today. Second, there is the division of qualitative analysis. Qualitative knowledge has been relegated to the backbenches of scientific research. It has been considered an inferior method of obtaining scientifically valid data from which to extrapolate one's ideas and support their theoretical hunches. However, qualitative methods are required within the clinical area, and can provide a strong basis from which to begin the process of theory building.

Quantitative analysis and statistics

Perhaps the most challenging area of study within the undergraduate program is that of statistics. For many students this can be a personal nightmare, yet I often wonder why this is the case. Is it perhaps that mathematics has always been presented to students in school as an unfathomable and mysterious challenge? An area of study that is serious, complicated and only for the 'brainy' ones, and so when they enter university the last thing they expect is that they will have to meet this challenge themselves?

Fortunately, there are many excellent computer software packages designed specifically for managing data files, so much of the trauma has been taken away. However, the student still needs to grapple with concepts such as psychometric properties — such as validity and reliability, dependent and independent variables, hypotheses and probability. Quantitative analysis is fundamental to psychology when it comes to developing measurement of behaviours, cognitions and emotions. Sometimes there is criticism about this area of work based on why such an empiricist mathematical approach to measuring constructs is used when these aspects are themselves not quantifiable. That is, while we talk of factors such as intelligence quotients, anger, fear, anxiety, depression, memory, and so on, it is impossible to identify these as concrete objects. But it is through the process of experimentation and statistical analysis that the psychologist attempts to provide a measure of relativity.

Take heart, there are many good basic books available to lead you along your way (check the appendix for some references which I have found helpful for students). Your lecturers and tutors will also have an excellent grounding in this subject and will be able to provide you with necessary guidance and support as you go. Whatever you do, do not undervalue or dismiss the importance of this aspect of your studies. To be able to read and understand others' research, to be able to be discriminating in your future practices, you need to have this basic understanding.

Aside from providing you with a framework from which to interpret the discipline of psychology, it will also provide you with a very solid foundation for making some strong and important life choices and practical decisions in your future life. Whether that is in determining appropriate schooling practices for your child, sorting through the latest market research or unravelling political discussion, this area of study is not irrelevant. Even if you decide that your future professional choice is not to be a psychologist, the time spent within this subject area will not be wasted.

Qualitative analysis

As noted previously, this aspect of research has been considered secondary to scientific research analysis. Indeed, still today there are only a few universities that provide qualitative studies in their undergraduate psychology degrees. Qualitative analysis has its foundations in less empirically dominated areas of research — it uses a more subjective than mathematical approach. It is the method of analysis favoured by Freud and others in their research. It is also often found in disciplines of study such as history, cultural studies, law and sociology.

Qualitative research is based on the development of theoretical ideas and knowledge through the application of case studies, interviews and fieldwork. This area of study helps the student learn about interviewing and case analysis. They study the intricacies of life as it is experienced by the individual, group or organisation, through the accounts of the individuals involved. They learn to analyse transcripts of data, to digest volumes of notes, and to develop an understanding of phenomena through the intense scrutiny of words, actions and events. For example, many accounts of the experiences of people following the US tragedy on September 11th 2001 were based on qualitative analysis. Similarly, many case reports of clients for court and educational purposes are from an educated account of their current situation. Often, however, these reports also include some empirical assessment of their current psychological functioning capacity as well.

While this area of analysis is becoming much more popular, and has appeal to the student, unfortunately it still has its detractors. While extensive work has been undertaken by proponents of this methodology to provide an empirical basis to their work, you will often come across issues related to trustworthiness, integrity and reflexivity. Fortunately, as with statistics, there are several good software packages now available for handling large amounts of qualitative data. However, in most instances these are not necessary for the beginning student.

Although many students often leap at the chance of doing qualitative research, often they are disillusioned to find it is not the 'soft' option they had hoped for. In fact, mastering qualitative research methodology is often much harder than the quantitative approach.

Report writing

Much of the work in psychology undergraduate studies involves research report writing. This involves the student learning the basics of conducting rigorous scientific research into issues associated with psychology. They are expected to learn how to locate and review current literature, develop hypotheses and conduct experiments associated with human development, cognitions, social psychology, development, and so on. Most work conducted at undergraduate level is quasi-experimental (resembling/simulated), although in some instances students do get to work in heavily controlled laboratory settings.

The student's role at this stage is to develop an understanding of the principles involved in conducting research, how to design a study and conduct the relevant analysis. Importantly, the student is also expected to make sense of their findings of such research and develop an expertise in presenting substantiated reports about the study and any intrinsic meanings they may have uncovered.

While students find this process all rather cumbersome and confusing, over the three years of their undergraduate studies this process helps them develop a basic template of how to conduct their own independent research and engage in thesis writing at higher levels. A basic template for report writing is included in the appendices. The fundamental reference for all writing in psychology is the *Publication Manual of the American Psychological Association* (APA manual).

Essay writing

An important aspect of undergraduate studies is learning the basics of academic writing through the process of essay writing. Generally the student is instructed to write an essay or literature review on a specific topic of current interest within the discipline. It is expected that the student will conduct their own research into collecting relevant literature, develop skills in critical analysis of previous literature and develop a comprehensive overview of the current state of knowledge. There are strict guidelines for formatting of all writing in psychology, and students are strongly urged to access an APA manual for guidance on referencing styles and formatting.

Critical analysis of previous work requires students to go beyond presenting a purely descriptive overview of the literature. Students need to be able to integrate all the information, highlight what is not known as much as what is known and expose limitations which appear to exist. This form of essay writing is very different from that learnt in secondary schooling, and removes the first person from the subject. Students must learn to be objective, to develop a keen understanding of the differing theoretical positions upon which ideas are based and start to formulate their own preferred position, that is, will they take a behaviouralist stance or a humanist stance? Will they be wary of anything that does not have sound scientific basis to support the evidence? Will they be critical of anything that is not empirically driven? Or will they support specific interests such as the para-normal or spirituality?

This is the perfect opportunity for the student to begin to refine their ideas and create their own foundations of knowledge for future work. There are some excellent web-based sites that provide assistance with developing these fundamental skills. Also refer to the reference list in the back of this book.

Assessment

Assessment is a very important aspect of psychological work and students generally do not begin this area of study until their third year. Students are introduced to some of the primary assessment tools available to the practitioner for evaluating a specific issue or concern. Intelligence tests are one of the foremost tools utilised by any psychologist, and students will learn about the development of this construct, how to apply the tests and evaluate differing aspects of intellectual functioning across the lifespan. Similarly, students will be exposed to neurological testing, group and individual testing of specific skills and personality (or individual differences as they are now known), and introduced to the concept of test development itself, report writing and ethical guidelines. Many students find this to be one of the most exciting aspects of their undergraduate study program, and finally feel as if they are doing something that is of interest to them. However, without having the background in research, essay and report writing already defined, it is unlikely that they would comprehend or enjoy this area of study as much. It is these other aspects of foundational study that empower the student to fully engage in the process of assessment and appreciate its utility.

Ethics

Ethics are those moral principles adopted in determining what is right and correct within a given situation. While they are usually informed by laws and professional guidelines, ethical behaviour is not specifically defined by either. The profession of psychology has a code of ethical conduct that applies to its members; similarly there are many laws and obligations attached to how one conducts themselves in relation to others. There are also social and cultural codes of conduct that need to be considered. Ethics as taught within psychology is based on ensuring that the practitioner or researcher does not intentionally nor unintentionally cause any unnecessary physical or psychological distress to another person. Therefore the student is taught the underlying principles of ethical behaviour for psychologists and trained to consider the application of their work from an ethical viewpoint. Most undergraduate work is conducted under the close supervision of a lecturer or tutor, who is responsible for ensuring high ethical standards are maintained. However, by fourth year the student is expected to have a solid understanding of what is and is not considered to be appropriate behaviour.

As a security measure, all university campuses and hospitals have an assigned board of ethics, which the intending researcher or practitioner is expected to consult prior to adopting some new method of treatment or research program. Similar committees and governance structures are also in place in most government organisations. Private organisations and individuals rely on high levels of personal integrity and/or consultation with their local registration board or professional association for advice. Remember, your registration is dependent upon your conduct as a professional psychologist, and complaints of unethical behaviour are taken seriously. It is not uncommon for a psychologist to be the recipient of complaints from their clients or research participants. It is up to you to ensure that you have at all times acted in an honest, trustworthy and ethically responsible manner. Being disbarred from practice is not an exciting option!

Putting it all together

As you can no doubt appreciate, the undergraduate component of psychology is a very complex and serious pursuit of study. You will have learnt much about the theoretical underpinning of the discipline itself; you will have learnt much about how the human psyche functions. You will know about cognitive and emotional development, you will have explored the workings of the brain, and examined issues of psychopathology, community development, lifespan development and social interaction. You will also have developed many skills that you can apply to a multitude of areas in your private and working life.

Now comes the tough part. What do you do with all this knowledge and expertise? For many of you, this is where it begins to unravel. It is often at this stage that I most often consult with students who have come to a major crossroad in their life. For many students three or four years of intensive study, coupled with working part-time, personal maturation and developing strong intimate relationships means that they are left wondering what to do next. Frequently the student has not been free from study for over 16 years of their life. If they haven't already, they are now seriously considering the options of independence. They desire the chance to move out of the family home, to earn a decent income and to 'live'.

Congratulations. You have made it to a very important place in your life path, and you are equipped with the fundamental skills and knowledge to pursue a diversity of occupations and careers. Some of you may have already transferred over, or be thinking of studying social work. Others will be more interested in advertising or market research. Some will choose to enter the profession of teaching. Still others will join the army, police force, administration or other organisational practices. Others may choose to apply for a graduate position with the public service or, if they haven't yet had the chance, some students decide that now is the time to take off. To explore the world and find their true selves. If you are in the least bit unsure about where or what you want to do, now is the time to seriously seek some assistance. Most universities offer counselling and vocational support for their students, and it is an ideal time to utilise this opportunity. Hopefully, many of you will already have accessed these services throughout your undergraduate years; however, it is never too late. If you are unsure ask your coordinator of studies for some referrals, and don't be too shy to discuss your concerns with your tutors and lecturers. They have been there; they know the process and are only too happy to assist you with accessing the necessary resources to help you work out your dilemmas. They are psychologists after all!

For the others, the students who know what they want — to become a psychologist — the next step on your journey is equally important. The minimum requirement for you to gain qualification as a psychologist is to complete a fourth year of accredited study and two years of supervised practice. However, if you feel like you need a break at this stage, do take it. It is possible to defer studies for another year, or indeed, go out and work for a while then return to study later when the timing is more applicable for you and your circumstances. In the next chapter, I will discuss the options of study available to the fourth-year student and also examine some of the possibilities for gaining supervised practice.

Becoming a Psychologist in Australia

Fourth year
and graduate studies

The fourth year of study is pivotal to the professional development of students wanting to become psychologists. As with the undergraduate years, this year is also one full of choices. Decisions need to be made whether to pursue an Honours degree or alternatively to opt for a Graduate Diploma in Psychology. Previously the choice was quite clear: an Honours degree was selected if postgraduate studies at a Masters or PhD level were being considered at a later date. Alternatively, for students returning to study or wanting to formalise qualifications after working within the area for some time, a Graduate Diploma specialising in their preferred area of study was a better option.

More recently, with accreditation of the educational basis of the profession the differences between these two fields of study changed. Presently there is little differentiation between an Honours course and a Graduate Diploma on the basis of study — the distinction is made purely on academic performance and economics.

Honours programs

Honours programs are considered to be for those students who have shown excellence in their undergraduate studies. An Honours degree is funded at the equivalence of undergraduate fees and is therefore quite costly for the institution to provide. Places within Honours programs are not automatically provided for everyone who wants to pursue them, but are allocated on a pro-rata basis according to undergraduate loads. Thus the student who is offered an Honours position is often one who has excelled at their undergraduate levels and indicated a high aptitude for further studies.

A number of universities do not take new students into their Honours programs, but reserve the places for their own cohort of students. It is a good idea to explore the options as there are a few universities who do make some provision for students who want to change their location and perhaps feel another university has more relevant areas of expertise or options for study.

Graduate Diploma of Psychology

An alternative choice to the Honours program for the budding psychologist is to enrol in a Graduate Diploma. The Graduate Diploma is very similar to an Honours degree with the differences being a slight discrepancy in the weighting of units of study, and study may involve one or two different areas of knowledge, rather than engaging in a theoretical reading group. The fees for a Graduate Diploma are calculated on past graduate studies and are therefore slightly higher than undergraduate studies. Fortunately, the Government has recognised the increased economic pressure this places on the student and has now provided an alternative fee payment plan to HECS known as Fee-help. I recommend you explore this option if necessary.

A Graduate Diploma is also an excellent option for students who have decided to return to study after several years of absence from formal study. It can often be undertaken part-time and is offered with consolidated hours of contact to enable one to also engage in paid work. While some consider the Graduate Diploma to be an inferior qualification, this is not necessarily the case. A student who does well in their studies and submits a top class thesis, whether Honours- or Graduate Diploma–based, has generally equal opportunity to enter further postgraduate studies.

A word of warning

For those who want to pursue a postgraduate scholarship in later studies, this is often not available to the Graduate Diploma student. Due to government restrictions of Research Training Scheme placements, the availability of scholarships has been severely cut. If you want to continue postgraduate study by research you need to really work hard from day one and seek Honours level in your studies. Similarly, it is imperative that if you are pursuing fourth-year studies with the intention of becoming a psychologist, you must ensure that your program is an accredited course of study.

While exploring all the offerings at this level you will note that there are many courses available in counselling, child and adolescent development, psychoanalysis, Gestalt, narrative therapy, and so on. While these courses in themselves are excellent avenues to explore and study, they are not necessarily aligned purely with psychology, nor are the entry requirements as strict. For anyone who is not concerned about having a professional registration as a psychologist, then these are potentially ideal. However, be warned, they may not be adequate levels of study for registration purposes.

Areas of study in fourth year

By the time you arrive at fourth year you are ready to enter the most exciting and challenging year of study. This is when you get the opportunity to take on the role of being a newcomer into the profession and display your talents as an intelligent, well-grounded and thoughtful scientist and potential practitioner.

Perhaps the biggest challenge for the fourth-year student is the thesis. You will be provided with the opportunity to extensively study a theoretical position within the discipline and write an extended piece or work in that area. Your expertise in research methodology will be extended, and your introduction to psychology as a profession begins in earnest.

Reading programs

Reading programs are offered to the student in a variety of discipline areas. In any one year one may be able to choose between neurology, clinical applications, memory, development or community psychology, to note just a few. Within this program the student is exposed to extensive theoretical and research-based literature within the specific areas and a variety of current applications of this literature to the practical world. It is the student's task, under close supervision from an adviser, to thoroughly investigate this literature and develop a comprehensive review of the evidence to argue a specific position. For example, you may be asked to discuss the relevance of community supports in enhancing rehabilitation following serious illnesses, or to discuss the evidence available to substantiate the introduction of early learning programs to enhance literacy in schools.

It is the student's task to write an informed, critical analysis of the available literature and provide a strong argument for their position. By utilising the skills from undergraduate essay writing classes a substantial, usually 5,000-word essay on their chosen topic will be developed. Often this is undertaken in small-group formats with up to 15 students exploring a similar area of theoretical knowledge and applying it to a range of current topics.

The thesis

At last, the opportunity to put all those years of report writing and analytical skills to the test, an opportunity for many budding psychologists to finally have their own input. The thesis will be your own large research report, a culmination of the three or more years of hard work and study. The student is solely responsible for generating the piece of research as the thesis conceptualises an idea and applies rigorous scrutiny.

Ideally this piece of work is conducted on an individual basis; however, in some universities students have the opportunity to link to current research being conducted within the organisation. Therefore if you have had the opportunity to develop a strong rapport and affinity with one of your lecturers now is the time for you to work collaboratively with him or her and possibly several other students in extending their research projects. You will be required to develop a sound theoretical basis for your ideas and then to engage in a substantial review of the literature and generate a solid research question. This step is significant and cannot be overlooked. The worst experiences I have had are when confronted with a student who has piles of data, three weeks before submission time, without any idea of why or what data they have collected. As you will have surely learnt by this stage in your development as a psychologist, any monkey can push buttons and generate a statistic; however, only a statistical analysis based on solid foundations is of any relevance.

From the solid research question, hypotheses are generated and a project is designed that will facilitate your data collection and outcomes. While some students opt for self-report style convenience sampling to conduct this part of their work, others engage in strict laboratory-based experimentation, or diverge into qualitative and field research. As I noted before, this is the time for you to make the choices about where you want to go and what areas of the discipline you want to invest your time and energy.

The thesis is generally around 10,000 words in length. Students work with the close supervision of a tutor or lecturer and are expected to consult with their supervisor consistently and honestly throughout their project. The supervisor is there to guide and advise; it is not their task to conceptualise, to analyse or to write the paper. Writing a thesis is an intense self-driven project and the pivotal point of all future studies and work; it will be the linchpin of all future studies and work so make it the central focus of your studies for the whole year.

Guidelines for writing the thesis are readily available; the thesis is an extension and application of all previous undergraduate studies and experience — enjoy the challenge.

Professional orientation

'Ahhhh! At last', I can hear some of you saying. 'A topic that may just address my concerns'. The professional orientation aspect of study in the fourth year brings together a consolidation of assessment practices along within an introduction into the varying pathways available in future professional life. This is when students begin to explore the differing fields of application of knowledge to the 'real world'. The fundamentals of private practice, organisational life and clinical application are explored. There are opportunities to attend lectures and seminars given by people who practice within the field. Many students undertake a project that involves going out into the field and shadowing a psychologist, or interviewing several psychologists within a division of psychology, and reporting back to their group on the specifics entailed in that area of work.

This is often the first time that some students will come into contact with psychologists outside of academia and is the opportunity to explore and develop a portfolio of interests and enhance future work opportunities. While it may seem a less intensive unit compared to the other academically driven tasks that you will undertake in this year of your studies, it may also be the most important formative process undertaken. Ethics, use of assessment tools and interpersonal interaction with clients are very serious components of future work.

Choices made at this time are important. It is no use ending up working in a clinical setting in a hospital if you really are interested in working with youth in a community environment. Similarly, if you are totally intrigued with the neurological functioning of the brain you will be utterly miserable if you end up working in human resource management. This is your opportunity to take the time to make those important decisions and consolidate your position.

Research methods

In fourth year your studies in statistics and qualitative analysis are consolidated. These studies also provide the opportunity to strengthen your thesis through engaging in this unit of study. There are opportunities to investigate multiple applications of research design and process to everyday matters — such as evaluation, intervention and prevention programs, as well as social and developmental issues. An extension of statistical capabilities is also offered, so that those who are interested in academic or applied areas of psychology can strengthen their skills and knowledge base in this region. On completing your fourth year you will be well prepared to engage in any tasks associated with higher levels of employment in whatever area you are interested, whether in the area of psychology or elsewhere.

Where to now?

Well here's the tricky bit. Just as you are coming to the climax of your studies, up jumps the next obstacle. Yes, right in the middle of your final year of study the impact of everything hits. What to do now? Where do you go? How do you decide? First there is the decision to make. Are my grades good enough to carry me further in academia? Do I really want to keep studying for another two, maybe three years? How can I afford it? Where do I find a job?

Volunteer work

Many students are pro-active in pursuing outside experiences and have had the opportunity to engage in some serious developmental work, through either paid employment or a voluntary capacity. For the majority it will have been voluntary. There are many excellent organisations around who provide opportunities for the interested layperson to engage in nominal 'psychologically' based work practices. First to mind come the telephone counselling services, but there are also school-based mentoring programs and hospital-care listings. Other students will have worked in aged-care settings, or the service industry. Do not underestimate the skills and knowledge that can be obtained through work outside of formal study.

If you haven't had the opportunity to engage in any externally based employment or volunteer work, now is definitely the time to start building up your résumé.

Employment

There are several organisations that offer internships to successful fourth-year students, particularly in the area of organisational work. Similarly, the state governments often employ students in their departments of human services. Both options also provide the new graduate with the necessary supervision they require for full registration. Alternatively, the Federal Government offers a restricted level of intake for postgraduate students into their branches of policy development, diplomacy, and so on. Perhaps your preference is to work in rural areas or with indigenous populations; others will want to diversify into environmental issues, animal welfare or even politics.

Résumé writing, employee applications, job hunting, scholarship applications, choosing to complete further studies in a specialist master's program — all require attention at this time. Alternatively, you may decide that this is the time to take a break, take time out, time to reflect, gather your resources and re-engage with life as you once knew it. Consult your careers officer at university, seek assistance from the counsellors and speak with your lecturers. Gather as much information as you can and make your decisions based on solid information.

Supervised practice

For some the choice is straightforward. They want to get their teeth into working in a paid capacity and now is the time when you can do just that. As a successful fourth-year candidate you are ready and equipped to enter into professional practice. At this stage, however, you are only eligible to register as a probationary psychologist. In order to earn your full registration you must undergo at least two years of supervised practice under the guidance of a registered psychologist. This process is quite enjoyable for some; however, others find it quite daunting and intimidating. Some find it difficult to enter into a work environment where they, once again, start out as the apprentice. However, this is not meant to be a demeaning process, but a practice set in place to ensure your own, as well as the public's, safety and wellbeing as you learn to negotiate the many hurdles and obstacles that arise within any work environment. More importantly, in the majority of cases you are placed in a position of making very serious judgment calls and decisions regarding people's lives. This should never be taken for granted or treated lightly. The responsibility is great and it is yours.

A good supervisor is required. You need to ensure that you find someone who you can work well with. Someone who has your interests at heart and is available on a regular, consistent basis to provide you with a space for debriefing, consultation, reflection and honing of skills. Often supervisors are provided within the organisation that employs you. Alternatively, you may choose to engage your own supervisor and arrange private consultations with them on a weekly basis. Private supervision is expensive (ranging from $80 to $150 per session); however, it is a worthwhile and valuable experience to have the opportunity to work with, and learn from, someone who knows their area and is generous with sharing their knowledge and skills in a non-patronising and educative manner.

Further information regarding suitable supervisors and supervision is freely available from your state registration branch or the APS. Talk to others in the profession, ask your supervisor at university or speak with the student careers officer. They will all have a wealth of information to offer you with regard to this area of your professional development.

More study

Perhaps you haven't had enough study yet? You still feel intrigued and have a burning desire to formally enter into a specific area of professional psychological practice. Perhaps you are so enthused by the discipline that you have decided that academic or research work is the one and only true path for you. Good for you, then now is the time to make those decisions. What is it about psychology that really gets you going? For anyone who thinks that it's the money or the credentials, forget it, you are definitely on the wrong path! To pursue further studies is not for the faint-hearted, nor for anyone who wishes to get rich quick, or at all. I can highly recommend it to anyone who enjoys studying and is keen to become truly immersed in his or her area of professional and discipline interest. But then I am one of those nuts who also loved maths and physics in secondary school!

4

The postgraduate years

O kay, you've made it through the major hurdles of study to enter the profession and now you need to decide what specialisation is for you. While some will choose to take a few years' break from formal study, others will decide to pursue further studies and specialise in a particular area.

Whether you are fresh out of fourth year, returning to study after a break, or changing your profession, when applying for entry into 5th and 6th years of study it is imperative to really reflect on what it is about psychology that particularly intrigues and motivates you. It is important to think very carefully and make an informed choice about the path of study that you undertake. Some may decide that research has appeal, perhaps entertaining ideas of becoming an academic. Others may choose neuropsychology or forensics, or perhaps more applied areas of study, including community, health or sports psychology. Primarily the choice relates to whether you want to continue with coursework, and complete a Masters or Doctorate by coursework — or alternatively enrol in a PhD and complete your studies by thesis.

The following section lists the areas of specialisation recognised within the Australian context, and provides a brief overview of each discipline. At the back of the book there is a listing of currently recognised institutions and universities offering these areas of study (of course these may change over time so always follow up with your own investigations). However, first I think it is helpful to review what is involved in each of the options discussed.

Master by Coursework (MPsych)

A Master by Coursework provides student with an opportunity to specialise in a specific area of psychological studies. This course of study invites them to explore the theoretical underpinning of their particular discipline, engage in supervised placements within two or three organisations relevant to their field and to conduct an extended piece of research relevant to their field. Sometimes this study is completed in two years full-time, but many students elect to work through the study on a part-time basis. One of the main reasons is that many need to generate an income at the same time as they study, particularly those returning to study who also have family responsibilities.

Perhaps one of the most contentious areas within the master's program is with supervised placements. Sometimes students feel they are being exploited, purely because they are still offering their services without cost. This is not necessarily the case. The option of engaging in supervised work within different organisations is expensive for both the university and the organisation. Supervision is costly, so are many of the necessary infrastructure arrangements. The coordinator of programs within the university has a major task in overseeing the development and safety of the student, as well as the educational requirements being satisfied. Therefore, while the student does appear to be providing their services without remuneration there would be substantial costs to them involved if undertaking this placement outside of this framework.

A Masters program of study can be enjoyable, but it does require a major input of time and energy. The thesis component of the program is substantial and students need to engage in this from the first instance and work through it consistently. I have often found that this is the one area where students get into difficulties. They relish the opportunity to put their knowledge and skills into practice; they enjoy the heady intellectual pursuit and often put their thesis aside. There is nothing worse than getting to the end of three or four years of extended study to find you still have a major piece of work to complete. Without this being successfully completed, there is no potential for graduation. Successful completion of your Masters program makes you eligible for registration as a psychologist and also membership of the designated APS college (once a further 80 hours of professional development has been completed).

The Master by Coursework programs are not HECS funded, but are covered by Fee-help (a comparable student loans scheme for postgraduate students). Unfortunately, scholarships for this level of coursework are rarely available and students need to be financially prepared for the impact of studying. Completion of a Masters program is of serious benefit to the student and provides them with a substantial in-depth understanding and foundation for their future work. If you can, I recommend that you seriously consider taking up this option at some stage in your career.

Professional doctorate (DPsych)

A professional doctorate is the highest academic qualification available to the practitioner who would prefer to complete practical application and theoretical studies as a component of their overall studies, in comparison to those who engage in a PhD. The professional doctorate is an extension of the Master by Coursework, and includes further hours of supervised placement, coursework and a substantial research project.

While the current pay schedules for psychologists do not necessarily acknowledge having completed work beyond the level of a Masters degree, it may make the difference in terms of competition for employment.

As with the Masters programs, doctorates do not normally qualify for scholarship, but are covered by the Fee-help system. A cautionary note: the majority of universities do not appreciate students taking extended time to complete their thesis and students often find they are required to pay large amounts to continue their studies over and above the prescribed time. Often this can amount to $2,500 per term for supervision while they are writing up their thesis.

Serious consideration must be given to both the pros and cons involved in taking up this extra year of study option, if it is offered. Unless you have guaranteed income and potential for secure employment, there is a high possibility that the expense incurred may never be recouped. However, some will be satisfied to pay this money purely for the pleasure and enjoyment of the process itself.

Doctor of Philosophy (PhD)

The PhD reflects a different educational pathway and to enrol in a PhD means committing yourself to three years of independent research work, under the close supervision of an adviser within your university. Sometimes this supervisor will be the only person you work with; however, there are instances when joint supervisory arrangements are made — usually because the area of specialisation requires differing input for theoretical understanding, analysis, and possibly conceptual development.

To enrol in a PhD means that you are proposing to complete a relevant piece of research that not only contributes to the area of knowledge under investigation, but also has significance to the broader community. The thesis is completely your own piece of work: you are responsible for its conceptualisation, development, implementation and completion. A PhD thesis can often be an offshoot from your fourth-year piece of work and builds on all previous lab reports completed in undergraduate study. To be accepted for candidature as a PhD student requires you to have a strong performance, and have indicated a significant aptitude for undertaking the task at hand. A PhD student is expected to be self-motivated, open to supervision and capable of conducting their work in a timely, intelligent and thoughtful manner.

Enrolment for PhD or Master by Research occurs simultaneously with an application for scholarship. While scholarships are very limited, many students receive awards to cover their fees. Availability of PhD places have been severely constrained in the past five years, so the first attempt may not necessarily succeed. Sometimes students need to go out and work on their ideas for a while, developing a stronger sense of their professional orientation. This places them in a much stronger position to engage in and succeed in the task at hand. With the tightening of government legislation surrounding postgraduate education, timelines for completion of a PhD have also been limited. In the past students may have written their PhD over a 10- or 12-year period, but this is no longer an option. Time frames now require students to have submitted their work within three years. Funding of placements is highly contingent on universities ensuring their students do submit on time, and there may be large financial implications outside of these limits. Similarly, it may mean that succeeding placements for future students will be removed. The onus is therefore on the candidates to make sure they engage, receive and utilise the resources provided and learn to self-motivate themselves. This is an apprenticeship into an academic life, and it requires independence and responsibility on the students' behalf if they wish to succeed.

Apart from the obvious difficulties students encounter — such as taking themselves seriously, working continuously without external impositions, and juggling outside work commitments, family and relationship issues — perhaps the toughest component of the task is negotiating supervision. Supervision, in this context, is vastly different to supervision while working with clients. Your supervisor should be a person whom you know well, at least academically, who has a high level of expertise in your proposed area and has indicated a strong interest in taking you on as their student. Your supervisor is there to assist you through the process, to facilitate your reading, provide directions on how to structure and develop your project and ensure the appropriate ethical and professional standards are maintained. The university generally allocates your supervisor an amount of teaching time per week to engage in discussions with you. They will also be available for reading drafts of work, consultation on analysis and assistance networking with outside organisations as required.

However, the supervisor is not responsible for ensuring you actually use these resources. Often I meet students who are floundering in the last stages of their candidature, only to find that they have not utilised this process very well. Perhaps they started out with a couple of weekly, or in some cases monthly, consultations with their supervisor, then other extraneous matters catch up with them and they fall further and further behind. This is when it becomes a matter of balance and prioritising all aspects of life.

Conducting a major research project requires a continuous process of writing, researching, data collection and analysis. It is not okay to just get a good idea, collect some data and then try to create a document out of it. Writing and editing the final piece takes a considerable amount of time and persistence and cannot be completed in a couple of weeks! One of the most significant pieces of advice I can offer you is that it is important that you ensure you have a productive relationship with your supervisor and make sure you utilise all the resources made available.

Apart from time management, relationship with your supervisor and utilising resources, you also need to develop excellent computer skills. If you have not already learnt how to utilise a library archive system to keep track of literature viewed, for example Endnote, now is a very good time to start. Electronic resourcing of literature and other materials is essential. While you will have developed very strong writing and grammatical skills during your studies, if it is a while since you have engaged in formal academic studies it is time to brush up on these. Because your PhD candidature will require you to make presentations, your interpersonal communication skills, use of PowerPoint for seminar and conference presentations and your own presentation skills, both physical and verbal, will need to be polished.

Engaging with the postgraduate studies unit within your university and participating in academic life beyond your own area of interest is important. It can become very lonely and isolating experience for the student who silently works away in an office or workplace. Try not to avoid interaction with your peers; they may have some valuable ideas and input into your work, and they are also experiencing comparable stresses and strains. They are also potentially your future colleagues, employees or employers.

For those who decide to undertake a PhD with the intent of becoming an academic you will also be offered the opportunity to take on minor tutoring tasks and, in later stages, even some lecturing of undergraduate students. I suggest that you take up the offer and try it. Some love it and it confirms their decision re the academic role. Others realise that face-to-face interaction with students is not for them and they redirect their energies into research opportunities.

Whatever direction you choose, congratulations, you have taken on a wonderful opportunity that can be a life-enhancing period. I trust it goes well and I look forward to hearing of many successes.

Areas of specialisation

Counselling psychology

The counselling psychologist specialises in working with individuals, families and groups in the context of interpersonal relationship issues, employment and career concerns, personal health and wellbeing, grief, trauma, and other life crises. The counselling psychologist is trained in various therapeutic techniques aimed at enhancing communication, assessment and treatment skills. Most of the work in this field is associated with managing everyday life issues for the individual, couple or group. Counselling psychologists are also trained to work with people who are undergoing recovery from illness and injury. They are often employed within community-centred organisations, schools and government services organisations.

Clinical psychology

The clinical psychologist specialises in working with people who are suffering from all aspects of psychopathology and poor mental health. The training for clinical psychologists is in assessment diagnosis and treatment of psychological dysfunction ranging from birth through older age (i.e., autism, schizophrenia, panic disorder, depression, Aspberger's syndrome, Alzheimer's, etc.). They are generally employed within hospital, general medical centres, community and mental health services. They often also work in case-mix environments alongside psychiatrists, medical practitioners and other para-professionals, as well as organisations involved in health promotion and prevention.

Clinical neuropsychology

The clinical neuropsychologist specialises in assessment, diagnosis and treatment of cognitive, emotional and behavioural problems associated with head trauma and brain injury. Generally employed in hospitals and rehabilitation centres, the neuropsychologist works with individuals who, through either birth or injury, have suffered cognitive impairment (i.e. stroke, epilepsy, dementia, head injury, learning difficulties, attention deficit disorder, etc.). Some neuropsychologists also specialise in research and program development for prevention of injury and disease (i.e., Transport Accident Commission, CSIRO, etc.).

Community psychology

The community psychologist has a specialist background in social, environmental, ecological and community development. The community psychologist generally works with groups within the local community or the broader socio-political sphere. Their work is less focused on individual health issues, but more on evaluation, program and policy development. Community psychologists are considered to be agents of change and are committed to the principles of equity, cultural diversity, transparency and flexibility within the social arena of life. They generally work in partnership with individuals, groups and organisations, across both rural and urban environments through local governments, educational settings, community health and other non-government agencies.

Educational and developmental psychology

Educational and developmental psychology is primarily concerned with understanding the human being as they develop across the lifespan. The educational and developmental psychologist specialises in working with cognitive, behavioural and social issues that may arise as a result of dysfunction in one's development. They are skilled in assessment, vocational guidance, career counselling, child and adolescent development, adult work and social issues, as well as general functioning and well-being. Primarily employed within educational organisations, but can also be located in community centres, early childhood centres, crèches and other non-government organisations.

Forensic psychology

Forensic psychologists are involved in applying their skills and knowledge to working within the legal and criminal justice systems. They are often employed within the justice system and work in correctional institutions, the court and public services of the government. Forensic psychologists work with both perpetrators and victims. Their role is to assess, diagnose and treat individuals who have come before the judiciary system or who have experienced some form of criminal behaviour. The forensic psychologist is also involved in consulting and developing intervention and remedial programs, as well as representation of clients in court.

Health psychology

Health psychology is primarily concerned with health promotion; however, the specialist in this area is also engaged in clinical health issues. Generally employed within the public health sector, health psychologists are also found in larger hospitals, rehabilitation and community health centres as well as health and policy organisations. The main focus of the health psychologist is on the promotion of healthy behaviours and intervention in non-healthy community practices. They work with individuals, groups and organisations in the treatment of psychosocial disorder and dysfunction, rehabilitation and mediation. Health psychologists are also involved in the development of treatment programs on both an individual and community level to help people deal with and prevent problems such as obesity, smoking, sexually transmitted disease, cardiac problems, and so on.

Organisational psychology

The organisational psychologist specialises in developing an informed understanding of workplace issues, organisational processes and individual health within the work environment. The organisational psychologist works with individuals, groups or organisations. They may be employed as human resource managers within the organisation, recruitment officers, career counsellors or occupational consultants. The organisational psychologist may also be employed on a consultancy basis within large corporations or business to evaluate current practices, train staff, or facilitate change. They can also be engaged in policy development, industrial dispute resolution and consumer advocacy.

Sports psychology

Sports psychology is heavily premised on the study of psychological and cognitive factors associated with physical activity, sports and exercise. The sports psychologist works with individuals and teams to facilitate healthy practices and enhance overall performance of athletes, sporting persons and individuals. They specialise in working with issues such as stress and time management, performance enhancement, anxiety management, relaxation and other cognitive skills (i.e., goal setting, imagery, confidence building), team building, leadership and rehabilitation.

Generalist psychology

The generalist psychologist is one who has completed their four years of training and then gained registration through supervised practice. The generalist psychologist can be found working within, or across, any of the identified specialist areas of psychology. In many instances, with appropriate supervision and continuing professional development, the general psychologist is as competent and informed as are their peers within a specific area of specialisation. However, ongoing competition and changes in employer expectations does seem to indicate that there is an increasing preference for someone who has had extended formal education when it comes to selection. There are no differing pay scales dependent on qualifications, but rather it is premised on experience. Moreover, often the psychologist will find that they are employed under differing awards, such as community development officer, social worker or counsellor, thus making any confirmed statements about remuneration rather difficult and complex. Suffice to say that if you are good at your work you are more likely to enjoy a long and productive career, with adequate remuneration. Remember that formal education is only one part of the puzzle; it is up to you as an individual to be prepared to develop your interpersonal skills, maintain a healthy lifestyle and work productively.

Private practice

Many psychologists opt for engaging in some form of private practice. Often this is in association with formal employment; however, there are those who work within their own private offices or with a team of others. Private practice is not for the faint-hearted and requires the development of excellent business management skills and engagement in extensive networking with colleagues, other professionals and the community. The cost of private consultancy is prohibitive for many individuals and therefore it can be a complex issue to build up one's practice. Medical rebates are not freely available and may be restricted to specific schedules and conditions and Medicare is not generally provided. However, those who choose to work in this manner are often quite pleased they took the risk and indicate a high level of personal as well as professional satisfaction. Remember, while there is a recommended schedule of fees for psychologists, you are often working in close competition with others who are not similarly qualified (anyone can put up a shingle and practice as a counsellor or psychotherapist). Unfortunately, outside of the profession there is still very little understanding of the differences between psychologists, counsellors and psychotherapists. Therefore your clients are often going to be quite reluctant to pay premium rates for your services until you have become firmly established.

CHAPTER 5

Where to find studies in psychology

Recognised institutions and universities offering APS accredited studies in psychology

Details in the following section regarding courses and centres were obtained from the websites for each organisation and were correct at the time of publication. Readers are encouraged to visit the websites to ensure that they obtain current information.

Accredited Graduate Diploma in psychological studies

VICTORIA
AUSTRALIAN CATHOLIC UNIVERSITY
– Grad Dip in Psychology

DEAKIN UNIVERSITY — ALL CAMPUSES
– Grad Dip in Psychological Studies
LA TROBE UNIVERSITY — ALBURY/WODONGA, BENDIGO & BUNDOORA CAMPUSES
– Grad Dip in Psychology

MONASH UNIVERSITY
– Grad Dip in Psychology

ROYAL MELBOURNE INSTITUTE OF TECHNOLOGY — BUNDOORA
– Grad Dip in Behavioural Science

SWINBURNE UNIVERSITY OF TECHNOLOGY — LILYDALE
- Grad Dip in Soc Sci (Psychological Studies)

UNIVERSITY OF BALLARAT
- Grad Dip in Psychology

UNIVERSITY OF MELBOURNE
- Grad Dip in Psychology

VICTORIA UNIVERSITY
- Grad Dip in Psychological Studies

NEW SOUTH WALES

CHARLES STURT UNIVERSITY — BATHURST
- Grad Dip of Psychology

MACQUARIE UNIVERSITY
- Grad Dip of Psychology

SOUTHERN CROSS UNIVERSITY
- Grad Dip in Psychology

UNIVERSITY OF NEW ENGLAND
- Grad Dip Social Science

UNIVERSITY OF SYDNEY — BANKSTOWN, HAWKESBURY & PENRITH
CAMPUSES
- Grad Dip in Psychology

QUEENSLAND

BOND UNIVERSITY
- Grad Dip in Psychology

CENTRAL QUEENSLAND UNIVERSITY
- Grad Dip in Psychology

QUEENSLAND UNIVERSITY OF TECHNOLOGY
- Grad Dip in Psychology

UNIVERSITY OF SOUTHERN QUEENSLAND
- Grad Dip in Psychological Studies

SOUTH AUSTRALIA

FLINDERS UNIVERSITY OF SOUTH AUSTRALIA
- Grad Dip in Psychology

WESTERN AUSTRALIA

EDITH COWAN UNIVERSITY
- Grad Dip in Psychology

NORTHERN TERRITORY

CHARLES DARWIN UNIVERSITY
- Grad Dip in Psychology

Accredited 4th year programs

VICTORIA
AUSTRALIAN CATHOLIC UNIVERSITY
  – BA (Hons), BSocSci (Hons), BAppSci (Hons), Postgraduate Diploma in Psychology

DEAKIN UNIVERSITY — BURWOOD & GEELONG CAMPUSES
  – BA (Hons Psych), BSc (Hons Psych), BAppSc (Psych) (Hons)

DEAKIN UNIVERSITY — BURWOOD CAMPUS
  – Grad Dip Psych

LA TROBE UNIVERSITY
  – BBehSc (Hons), Post Grad Dip in Psychology

MONASH UNIVERSITY
  – BSc (Hons), BA (Hons), BBehNeurosc (Hons), PostGradDipPsych

ROYAL MELBOURNE INSTITUTE OF TECHNOLOGY — BUNDOORA
  – BAppSc (Psych) Hons, Grad Dip In Psych

SWINBURNE UNIVERSITY OF TECHNOLOGY — HAWTHORN
  – BA (Hons), Postgraduate Diploma of Psychology

UNIVERSITY OF BALLARAT
  – BA (Hons) Psych, Postgraduate Diploma of Psychology

UNIVERSITY OF MELBOURNE
  – BSc (Hons), BA (Hons), BComm (Hons), Postgraduate Diploma in Psychology

VICTORIA UNIVERSITY
  – BA (Hons), BSc (Hons), Graduate Diploma in Applied Psychology

NEW SOUTH WALES
CHARLES STURT UNIVERSITY — BATHURST
  – BSocSc (Psych) (Hons), Postgrad Diploma in Psychology

CHARLES STURT UNIVERSITY — WAGGA WAGGA
  – BA (Psych) (Hons)

MACQUARIE UNIVERSITY
  – BA-Psych (Hons), BSc-Psych (Hons), Post Grad Dip Psych

SOUTHERN CROSS UNIVERSITY
  – Postgraduate Diploma of Psychology

UNIVERSITY OF NEWCASTLE
  – BA (Hons), BSc (Hons)

UNIVERSITY OF NEW ENGLAND
  – BA (Hons), BSc (Hons), BSocSc (Hons)

UNIVERSITY OF NEW SOUTH WALES
  – BSc (Hons), BPsych (Hons)

UNIVERSITY OF SYDNEY
  – BA (Hons), BEcon (SocSc) (Hons), BSc (Hons), BLiberalStudies (Hons), Graduate Diploma in Science (Psych)

UNIVERSITY OF WESTERN SYDNEY — BANKSTOWN
  – BA (Hons), BAppSc (Hons), BPsych (Hons), BSocSc (Hons), Post Grad Dip of Psych

UNIVERSITY OF WESTERN SYDNEY — HAWKESBURY, PARRAMATTA, PENRITH
– Post Grad Dip of Psych

UNIVERSITY OF WOLLONGONG
– BA (Hons), BSc (Hons), Post Grad Dip Psych

QUEENSLAND
BOND UNIVERSITY
– BSocSc (Psych) (Hons), Postgraduate Diploma of Psychology

CENTRAL QUEENSLAND UNIVERSITY
– BA (Hons), Post Grad Dip Psych

GRIFFITH UNIVERSITY — GOLD COAST
– BPsych (Hons), Graduate Diploma of Psychology

GRIFFITH UNIVERSITY — MT GRAVATT
– Graduate Diploma of Psychology

JAMES COOK UNIVERSITY — CAIRNS & TOWNSVILLE
– Post Grad Dip of Psych

QUEENSLAND UNIVERSITY OF TECHNOLOGY
– BPsych (Hons), Postgraduate Diploma of Psychology

UNIVERSITY OF QUEENSLAND
– BA (Psych) (Hons), BSc (Psych) (Hons), BA (Hons) (Psych/CogSc), BA (Hons), (Psych/Human Mvmt), BPsychSc (Pass/Hons)

UNIVERSITY OF SOUTHERN QUEENSLAND
– BSc (Hons)

SOUTH AUSTRALIA
FLINDERS UNIVERSITY OF SOUTH AUSTRALIA
– BA (Hons), BSc (Hons), BBehSc (Hons)

UNIVERSITY OF ADELAIDE
– BA (Hons), BSc (Hons)

UNIVERSITY OF SOUTH AUSTRALIA
– BPsych (Hons)

WESTERN AUSTRALIA
CURTIN UNIVERSITY OF TECHNOLOGY
– BSc (Hons), BPsych (Graduate), Post Grad Dip Psych

EDITH COWAN UNIVERSITY
– BA (Hons), BSc (Hons), Post Grad Dip Psych

MURDOCH UNIVERSITY
– BA (Psych) (Hons)

UNIVERSITY OF WESTERN AUSTRALIA
– BPsych, BA (Hons), BSc (Hons) (Psych)

NORTHERN TERRITORY
CHARLES DARWIN UNIVERSITY
– BBehSc (Hons)

Becoming a Psychologist in Australia

TASMANIA
UNIVERSITY OF TASMANIA — HOBART
- BA (Hons), BSc (Hons)
UNIVERSITY OF TASMANIA — LAUNCESTON
- BA (Hons), BComm (Hons), BSc (Hons)

ACT
AUSTRALIAN NATIONAL UNIVERSITY
- BA (Hons), BPsych (Hons), BSc (Hons), BSc (Psych) (Hons), Graduate Diploma in Psychology
UNIVERSITY OF CANBERRA
- BAppPsych (Hons), Post Grad Dip in Applied Psychology

Accredited Masters programs

VICTORIA
AUSTRALIAN CATHOLIC UNIVERSITY
- MPsych (Child & Family), MPsych (Clinical), DPsych (Child & Family), DPsych (Clinical)
DEAKIN UNIVERSITY — BURWOOD CAMPUS
- MPsych (Clinical), MPsych (Forensic), MPsych (Health), DPsych (Clinical), DPsych (Forensic), DPsych (Health)
DEAKIN UNIVERSITY — GEELONG CAMPUS
- MIndustrial&OrgPsych
LA TROBE UNIVERSITY
- MPsych (ClinPsych), MPsych (ClinNeuropsych), MPsych (HealthPsych), MPsych (CounsPsych), DPsych (ClinPsych), DPsych (ClinNeuropsych), DPsych (HealthPsych), DClinicalPsych, DHealthPsych, DClinNeuropsych
MONASH UNIVERSITY
- MPsych (Couns), MPsych (Ed&Dev), MPsych (Health), MPsych (Org), DPsych (Clin), DPsych (ClinNeuro), DPsych (Org)
ROYAL MELBOURNE INSTITUTE OF TECHNOLOGY — BUNDOORA
- MPsych (Clinical), DPsych (Clinical), PhD (Clinical), MPsych (Ed&Dev), DPsych (Ed&Dev), PhD (Ed&Dev)
SWINBURNE UNIVERSITY OF TECHNOLOGY
- MPsych (Couns Psych), MPsych (Health Psych), DPsych (Couns Psych), DPsych (Health Psych)
UNIVERSITY OF BALLARAT
- DPsych (Clinical), DPsych (Health)
UNIVERSITY OF MELBOURNE
- MPsych (Org/Industrial), MPsych (Clinical), MPsych (ClinNeuropsych), MPsych (Ed Psych), DPsych (Clinical), DPsych (Child Clinical), DPsych (ClinNeuropsych), DPsych (Ed Psych), DPsych (Health), DPsych (Org/Industrial), MPsych (Org/Ind) / PhD, MPsych (ClinNeuro) / PhD, MPsych (Clinical) / PhD
VICTORIA UNIVERSITY
- MPsych (Clinical), MAppPsych (Community), MAppPsych (Sport), DPsych (Clinical),

NEW SOUTH WALES

CHARLES STURT UNIVERSITY — BATHURST
– MPsych (Clinical), MPsych (Forensic), DPsych (Clinical), DPsych (Forensic)

MACQUARIE UNIVERSITY
– MClinPsych, MCounsPsych, MClinNeuro, MOrgPsych, DPsych (ClinPsych), DPsych (ClinNeuro), DPsych (OrgPsych), DPsych (CounsPsych), PhD/MClinPsych, PhD/MCounsPsych, PhD/MClinNeuro, PhD/MOrgPsych

UNIVERSITY OF NEWCASTLE
– MAppPsych, MPsych (Clinical), MHealthPsych, MClinicalPsych, PhDHealthPsych, PhDClinicalPsych

UNIVERSITY OF NEW ENGLAND
– MPsych (Clinical), DPsych (Clinical)

UNIVERSITY OF NEW SOUTH WALES
– MPsych (Clinical), MPsych (Organisational), MPsych (Forensic), MPsych/PhD (Clinical), MPsych/PhD (Organisational), MPsych/PhD (Forensic)

UNIVERSITY OF SYDNEY
– DClinPsych/MSc, DClinPsych/PhD

UNIVERSITY OF WESTERN SYDNEY — BANKSTOWN
– MPsych (Clinical), MPsych (Ed&Dev), MPsych (Forensic), MPsych (Sport)

UNIVERSITY OF WESTERN SYDNEY — PENRITH
– MPsych (Ed&Dev)

UNIVERSITY OF WOLLONGONG
– MPsych (Clinical), DPsych (Clinical), PhD (Clinical)

QUEENSLAND

BOND UNIVERSITY
– MPsych, MPsych (Clinical), DPsych (Clinical)

GRIFFITH UNIVERSITY — GOLD COAST
– MClinPsych, MOrgPsych, PhD (Clinical), PhD (Org)

GRIFFITH UNIVERSITY — MT GRAVATT
– MClinPsych, MOrgPsych, PhD (Clinical), PhD (Org)

JAMES COOK UNIVERSITY — TOWNSVILLE
– MPsych (Clinical), DPsych (Clinical)

QUEENSLAND UNIVERSITY OF TECHNOLOGY
– MCounsPsych

UNIVERSITY OF QUEENSLAND
– MClinPsych, MPsych (Clin Neuro & Clin Psych), MEdPsych, MOrgPsych, MSport&ExerPsych, DClinPsych, DEdPsych, PhD (Clinical), PhD (Clin Neuro & Clin Psych), PhD (Educational), PhD (Organisational)

UNIVERSITY OF SOUTHERN QUEENSLAND
– MPsych (Health), MPsych (Sport & Exercise), DPsych (Health), DPsych (Sport & Exercise)

SOUTH AUSTRALIA

FLINDERS UNIVERSITY OF SOUTH AUSTRALIA
– Mpsych (Clinical), PhD (Clinical)

UNIVERSITY OF ADELAIDE
– Mpsych (Clinical), Mpsych (Org)

UNIVERSITY OF SOUTH AUSTRALIA
– Mpsych (Clinical), Mpsych (Forensic), Mpsych (Organisational), Mpsych
(Specialisation) (6 year sequence), DPsych (Clinical), DPsych (Forensic),
DPsych (Organisational)

WESTERN AUSTRALIA

CURTIN UNIVERSITY OF TECHNOLOGY
– Mpsych (Clinical), Mpsych (Counselling), Mpsych (Org)

EDITH COWAN UNIVERSITY
– Mpsych (Clinical & Clinical Geropsychology), Mpsych (Community
& Environmental), Mpsych (Forensic), DPsych (Clinical & Clinical
Geropsychology), DPsych (Forensic), DPsych (Community
& Environmental) PhD (Clinical & Clinical Geropsychology),
PhD (Community & Environmental), PhD (Forensic)

MURDOCH UNIVERSITY
– MAppPsych (Clinical), MAppPsych (Occupational), DPsych (Clinical),
DPsych (Occupational)

UNIVERSITY OF WESTERN AUSTRALIA
– Mpsych (Clinical), Mpsych/PhD (Clin), Mpsych (Clin Neuro), Mpsych/PhD
(Clin Neuro), Mpsych (App Dev), Mpsych/DipEd, Mpsych/PhD (App Dev),
Mpsych (Ind&Org), Mpsych/PhD (Ind&Org)

TASMANIA

UNIVERSITY OF TASMANIA
– Mpsych (Clinical), DPsych (Clinical), PhD (Clinical Psych), Mpsych
(Ed&Dev), DPsych (Ed&Dev), PhD (Ed&Dev)

ACT

AUSTRALIAN NATIONAL UNIVERSITY
– MClinPsych, DClinPsych, PhD (Clin Psych)

UNIVERSITY OF CANBERRA
– MAppPsych (Counselling)

Alternative psychology-related qualifications (non-APS accredited) in Australia

PSYCHOTHERAPY AND COUNSELLING

PSYCHOTHERAPY AND COUNSELLING FEDERATION
OF AUSTRALIA (PACFA)
PO Box 481 Carlton South, Vic 3053
E-mail: admin@pacfa.org.au
Website: www.pacfa.org.au

The Psychotherapy and Counselling Federation of Australia, Inc. (PACFA) is an 'umbrella' association comprising affiliated professional associations that represent various modalities within the disciplines of Psychotherapy and Counselling in the Australian community.

The 40 PACFA member associations incorporate a wide range of modalities within the fields of counselling and psychotherapy; in fact, this broad range along the continuum is part of what gives PACFA its strength and credibility. PACFA has been able to unite professionals from this wide range and give them a voice and presence.

The PACFA member associations have all been audited by the PACFA Management Committee and have met the minimum requirements in three different and distinct areas: Structure, Training and Ethics.

Member associations

Adelaide Institute for Psychoanalysis, Association of Personal Counsellors Inc., Association of Solution Oriented Counsellors and Hypnotherapists of Australia, Australian and New Zealand Association of Psychotherapy (NSW Branch), Australian and New Zealand Psychodrama Association Inc., Australian and New Zealand Society of Jungian Analysts, Australian Association of Group Psychotherapists, Australian Association of Marriage and Family Counsellors, Australian Association of Somatic Psychotherapists, Australian Association of Spiritual Care and Pastoral Counselling, Australian Centre for Psychoanalysis, Australian College of Psychotherapists, Australian Hypnotherapists Association, Australian National Art Therapy Association, Australian Radix Teachers Association, Australian Somatic Integration Association, Christian Counsellors Association of Australia Inc., Clinical Counsellors Association, Counselling and Psychotherapy Association Canberra and Region, Counselling Association of South Australia Inc., Counsellors And Psychotherapists Association of NSW Inc., Counsellors And Psychotherapists Association of Victoria Inc., Dance Therapy Association of Australia, Emotional Release Counsellors Association of NSW, Gestalt Australia and New Zealand, Institute of Clinical Psychotherapy Inc., Melbourne College of Contemporary Psychotherapy, Melbourne Institute for Experiential and Creative Arts

Therapy, Melbourne Institute for Psychoanalysis, Music and Imagery Association of Australia, New South Wales Family Therapy Association, NSW Institute of Family Psychotherapy, Professional Counsellors Association of Tasmania, Psychoanalytic Psychotherapy Association of Australasia, Psychotherapists and Counsellors Association of WA, Queensland Association for Family Therapy, Queensland Counsellors Association Inc., Queensland Transpersonal and Emotional Release Counsellors Association Inc., Society of Counselling and Psychotherapy Educators, Sydney Institute for Psychoanalysis, Victorian Association of Family Therapists, Victorian Child Psychotherapists Association, Western Pacific Association of Transactional Analysis.

PSYCHOANALYSIS

THE AUSTRALIAN PSYCHOANALYTICAL SOCIETY
PO Box 753,
Hawthorn East, 3122
E-mail: king@hyp.com.au
Website: www.psychoanalysis.asn.au

A component society of the International Psychoanalytical Association, the Australian Psychoanalytic Society has branches in Sydney, Adelaide and Melbourne.

The International Psychoanalytical Association has 11,000 members in 34 countries and works with component societies to provide standards of training, conferences, international congresses, and to develop clinical, education and research programs. As a component society, the Australian Psychoanalytical Society is the only body in Australia authorised by the IPA to educate, train and qualify psychoanalysts.

MELBOURNE BRANCH
Website: www.psychoanalysis.asn.au/melbourne/
The training course now offered by the Melbourne Branch of the Australian Psychoanalytical Society is for applicants interested in qualifying as psychoanalysts and in practising in this capacity. Those accepted for training are mostly university graduates from the professions of psychology, social work and psychiatry, with the occasional candidate from another background. The usual age of people beginning the training is between 30 and 40. The training has as its main elements a personal analysis which begins prior to a candidate starting seminars and continues at least until qualification, a period of Infant Observation, a four-year program of theoretical and clinical seminars, and supervised psychoanalysis of at least two patients.

The Sydney Branch of the Australian Psychoanalytical Society is offering a training course for those interested in qualifying as psychoanalysts. Further training in child psychoanalysis is available during or after completion of the adult training.

The training consists of:

1. A personal analysis with an analyst authorised by the Australian Psychoanalytical Society.
2. Supervised clinical work with patients.
3. Seminars over a period of four years covering the main theoretical and technical areas of psychoanalysis today.

Applicants are eligible if they have a university degree or an equivalent acceptable to the Australian Psychoanalytical Society.

ADELAIDE BRANCH
Website: www.aipsych.org.au
In addition to formal analytic training, a Graduate Diploma in Psychotherapy is offered to suitably qualified candidates, as an alternative through the University of Adelaide. Many analysts as well as general psychiatrists with an interest in psychotherapy are involved in teaching this two-year course. Formal training in Child or Group Analysis is not currently available in Adelaide; these would require regular visits to Sydney or Melbourne.

Master of Psychoanalysis (Melbourne and Sydney)

This part-time postgraduate course offers a rigorous program of clinical studies and research in psychoanalysis at an advanced level. It is aimed at professionals and students in the field of mental health (psychologists, psychiatrists, psychotherapists, psychiatric social workers, psychiatric nurses, counsellors and others) and students and workers in disciplines that incorporate psychoanalytic knowledge and methodology (Philosophy, Women's Studies, Cultural Studies, History, Literature, Sociology, Anthropology, Education, Social Work and others). It involves the critical study of psychoanalytic theory and technique in its clinical applications, as well as the use of psychoanalysis in social sciences and the arts. The clinical components of the program focus on practical technical issues, diagnostic questions and the direction of the treatment. The teaching staff is a team of psychoanalysts and scholars of psychoanalysis with many years of experience in the postgraduate courses offered by the Australian Centre for Psychoanalysis.

In Melbourne, the Master of Psychoanalysis course is based at the St Albans Campus of Victoria University. This is located a short drive from the city and offers excellent facilities. Subjects will be offered in the evening, with the possibility of some Saturday workshops. In Sydney, the course will be offered on 10 monthly intensive weekends at the rooms of the College of Psychiatrists in Rozelle.

The course is recognised by the Australian Centre for Psychoanalysis as part of the training requirements (theoretical studies) in its program of training in psychoanalysis (personal analysis and clinical supervision are the two other major components of training). The course offers to professionals and trainees in the mental health field a sound conceptual basis for clinical psychoanalytic practice. This course is not intended to meet APS requirements for a professional psychology qualification.

A degree in a relevant discipline from an approved tertiary institution, or equivalent. Selection will be based on relevant professional and/or academic experience, referees' reports and interviews.

GESTALT THERAPY
GESTALT AUSTRALIA AND NEW ZEALAND
E-mail address: hmdiack@bigpond.com
Website: www.ganz.org.au
A PACFA member

Gestalt therapy is a growth-based approach that values self-awareness and self-responsibility in living. Its practice enhances people's capacity to make creative and adaptive choices in their lives. It is a holistic approach that integrates human functioning as well as considering a person's living environment, culture, individual development and history. The Gestalt approach is useful in helping people with a range of concerns, including relationship problems, unhappiness and depression, anxiety, life stress and discontent, difficulties in living and working with others, and past physical and emotional trauma. It is an approach that is of particular interest to people wanting self-exploration and personal development. The Gestalt practitioner relates with a client in a dialogical way, respecting personal boundaries and valuing liveliness and immediate responsivity. The focus in therapy is on identifying and describing a client's unique experience and meaning making, rather than interpreting and generalising. The Gestalt therapist offers a sensitive balance of support and challenge in assisting clients to explore their concerns and the difficulties they experience in realising their hopes. It is a process that includes creative experiments, which allow clients to explore and experience new options in living and being in the world. Gestalt practitioners work in many settings, including private and agency clinics and health services, as well as educational, organisational, community and personal development settings. But, in whatever context they work, Gestalt practitioners remain committed to a common perspective of valuing personal awareness and healthy relating.

ART THERAPY

AUSTRALIAN NATIONAL ART THERAPY ASSOCIATION
Phone number: 1300 557 002
E-mail address: secretary@anata.org.au
Website: http://www.anata.org.au

The Australian National Art Therapy Association Inc. (ANATA) is a non-profit organisation, founded in 1987, that has developed because of a growing interest in Art Therapy in Australia. There is an increasing number of Art Therapists in Australia who have completed a recognised, postgraduate training that meets professional standards. Current membership is approximately 250, including Professional, Contributing, Associate, Trainee and Student members.

Art Therapy involves the use of various art forms such as drawing, painting and sculpture in a therapeutic setting. It differs from traditional art in that the emphasis is on the process of creating, rather than on the end product. It is important to note that having a talent for art is not necessary to benefit from Art Therapy. The symbolic and metaphoric quality of art imagery and the focus on imaginative expression is used to encourage the client to explore ideas, feelings and issues evoked by the art-making process. This process allows for distance and objectivity and a space to see the many dimensions of an issue without being restricted by the linear form of verbal language.

Art Therapy training is at postgraduate level. There are three courses in Australia offering studies in Art Therapy at Masters degree level that meet the ANATA Training Guidelines. These are in Perth, Sydney and Melbourne. The formal prerequisite for training is a relevant degree in Visual Art or other degree equivalent. Training is intended for mature people who have work experience in rehabilitative and counselling settings and a demonstrated understanding of their own personal development through art-making processes. ANATA is actively working on clinical issues and professional development through establishing standards for Art Therapy training, registration and practice. ANATA offers support to Art Therapy professionals and others interested in this field by providing information on research, employment, standards, education and publications.

HYPNOTHERAPY

AUSTRALIAN HYPNOTHERAPISTS ASSOCIATION
Membership Enquiries: Bruni Brewin
Phone number: 1800 067 557
E-mail address: bruni_brewin@froggy.com.au
Website: www.ahahypnotherapy.org.au

The Australian Hypnotherapists Association (AHA) represents only professional clinical hypnotherapists. It was founded in 1949 and incorporated in 1956, and its Memorandum and Articles of Association have been registered with the Australian Securities and Investment Commission. The AHA is a non-profit, democratic institution, and is independent of any academic or commercial interest. The AHA has established uniform standards for professional hypnotherapists.

The AHA administers a thorough assessment process for Clinical Membership that includes written, oral and practical examinations, based on its competency and proficiency standards relating to the theory and practice of hypnosis and hypnotherapy.

MARRIAGE AND FAMILY COUNSELLING
AUSTRALIAN ASSOCIATION OF MARRIAGE AND FAMILY COUNSELLORS
Membership Enquiries: Bob Palfreyman
Phone number: 1800 806 054
E-mail address: contact@aamfc.org.au
Website: www.aamfc.org.au

The Australian Association of Marriage and Family Counsellors is a professional association established in 1978 to promote standards of excellence in the specialised field of relationship counselling across Australia. It has approximately 500 members in all states and territories working in private practice, government funded and non-government agencies, government departments and educational institutions.

To become a Clinical Member a counsellor must meet the following requirements post-training: three years standing as a counsellor; 750 hours of clinical experience, which must include 500 hours of couple and/or family counselling; and 75 hours of supervision. Clinical Membership is based on the applicant's demonstrated ability to work effectively with couples and/or families and to integrate theory and practice. Members may use a range of therapeutic approaches.

JUNGIAN ANALYSTS
AUSTRALIAN AND NEW ZEALAND SOCIETY OF JUNGIAN ANALYSTS
Membership Enquiries: Pam D'Rozario
Phone number: 08 9451 9541
E-mail address: pam.drozario@bigpond.com
Website: http://www.skyboom.com/anzsja

Members of the Australian and New Zealand Society of Jungian Analysts are usually called analytical psychologists or Jungian analysts. They have been trained to help people engage with and consider those unconscious forces that affect everyone's life and relationships to some degree.

Their work is based on insights and theories about the nature of self, developed by Carl Gustav Jung and the growing group of post-Jungian practitioners. Clinical practice relies on closely attending to and interpreting a person's dreams and/or symbolic imagery, the way this material and other thoughts and feelings are expressed, and the nature of the transference dynamics encountered in the relationship with the analyst. Analytical psychologists are also attentive to the often unconscious psychological links between individuals and society, including the cultures of groups and institutions. This interest in understanding a person's context reflect CG Jung's observations about universal or 'archetypal' dynamics and themes, and the influence on any individual's psychology of what he called the 'collective unconscious'.

ANZSJA was established in 1978. As a professional society it is sensitive to the particularities of the Australian and New Zealand context, and is committed to maintenance of high standards of practice. Opportunities for training and continuing education, research and reflection are a particular priority for the Society. It is one of 38 worldwide member societies functioning under the aegis of the Zurich-based International Association of Analytical Psychologists.

NARRATIVE THERAPY
THE DULWICH CENTRE
Hutt St
PO Box 7192 Adelaide, South Australia 5000.
Ph: (61-8) 8223 3966
Fax: (61-8) 8232 4441
E-mail: dulwich@senet.com.au
Website: www.dulwichcentre.com.au

Narrative therapy is an approach to counselling and community work. It centres people as the experts in their own lives and views problems as separate from people. Narrative therapy assumes that people have many skills, competencies, beliefs, values, commitments and abilities that will assist them to reduce the influence of problems in their lives. The word 'narrative' refers to the emphasis that is placed upon the stories of people's lives and the differences that can be made through particular tellings and retellings of these stories. Narrative therapy involves ways of understanding the stories of people's lives, and ways of re-authoring these stories in collaboration between the therapist / community worker and the people whose lives are being discussed. It is a way of working that is interested in history, the broader context that is affecting people's lives and the ethics or politics of therapy. These are some of the themes which make up what has come to be known as 'narrative therapy'. Of course, different people engage with these themes in their own ways. Some people choose to refer to 'narrative practices' rather than 'narrative therapy' as they believe that the phrase 'narrative therapy' is somewhat limiting of an endeavour which is constantly changing and being engaged with in many different contexts. Dulwich Centre offers a range of training opportunities for practitioners wishing to learn more about narrative therapy and to develop their own skills at narrative practice.

How to be registered as a psychologist

Australian registration and professional membership for psychologists

AUSTRALIAN CAPITAL TERRITORY

PSYCHOLOGISTS BOARD OF THE ACT,
PO Box 976, Civic Square, ACT 2608
Registrar: Ms Kathleen Taylor
Tel: (02) 6205 1599
Fax: (02) 6205 1602
E-mail: kathleen.lee@act.gov.au
Website: www.health.act.gov.au/healthregboards

NEW SOUTH WALES

PSYCHOLOGISTS REGISTRATION BOARD,
PO Box K599,
Haymarket, NSW 1238
Secretary: Ms Mary Shanahan
Tel: (02) 9219 0211
Fax: (02) 9281 2030
E-mail: psychreg@doh.health.nsw.gov.au
Website: www.psychreg.health.nsw.gov.au

NORTHERN TERRITORY

THE PSYCHOLOGISTS BOARD OF NT,
GPO Box 4221,
Darwin, NT 0801
Registrar: Ms Julie Burrows
Tel: (08) 8999 4157
Fax: (08) 8999 4196
E-mail: healthprofessions.ths@nt.gov.au
Website: www.nt.gov.au/health/org_supp/prof_boards/health_allied.pdf

QUEENSLAND

THE PSYCHOLOGISTS BOARD OF QLD,
GPO Box 2438,
Brisbane, QLD 4001
Registrar: Ms Pauline Portier
Tel: (07) 3225 2529
Fax: (07) 3225 2527
E-mail: psychology@healthregboards.qld.gov.au
Website: www.psychologyboard.qld.gov.au

SOUTH AUSTRALIA

SOUTH AUSTRALIAN PSYCHOLOGICAL BOARD,
16 Norma Street,
Mile End, SA 5031
Registrar: Mr Peter Martin
Tel: (08) 8443 9669
Fax: (08) 8443 9550
E-mail: sapb@saboards.com.au
Website: www.sapb.saboards.com.au

TASMANIA

PSYCHOLOGISTS REGISTRATION BOARD,
GPO Box 1712,
Hobart, TAS 7001
Registrar: Mr David Wills
Tel: (03) 6231 3866
Fax: (03) 6231 3565
E-mail: prbtas@bigpond.com
Website Link:
www.dhhs.tas.gov.au/corporateinformation/legislation/index.html

VICTORIA

PSYCHOLOGISTS REGISTRATION BOARD OF VICTORIA,
PO Box 358 Collins Street West,
Melbourne, VIC 8007
CEO and Registrar: Mr Anthony Grigg
Tel: (03) 9629 8722
Fax: (03) 9629 8744
E-mail: registrar@psychreg.vic.gov.au
Website: www.psychreg.vic.gov.au

WESTERN AUSTRALIA
PSYCHOLOGISTS BOARD OF WA,
PO Box 263,
West Perth, WA 6872
Registrar: Mr Trevor Hoddy
Tel: (08) 9481 0977
Fax: (08) 9481 3686
E-mail: kfirth@mjwa.com.au
Website: www.psychboard.wa.gov.au

Professional membership

AUSTRALIAN PSYCHOLOGICAL SOCIETY
PO Box 38
Flinders Lane Post Office
Melbourne, VIC 8009
Tel: 1800 333 497
Fax: (03) 9663 6177
E-mail: contactus@psychology.org.au
Website: http://www.psychology.org.au/

ASSOCIATION OF PRIVATE PRACTISING PSYCHOLOGISTS (QLD) INC.
PO Box 141
Sandgate, QLD 4017
Tel: 1800 802 554
Website: http://www.apppq.org.au/

AUSTRALIAN COUNSELLING ASSOCIATION
Suite 4/638 Lutwyche Road
Lutwyche, QLD 4031
Tel: (07) 3857 8288
Fax: (07) 3857 1777
E-mail: aca@theaca.net.au
Website: http://www.theaca.net.au/

International registration and professional membership for psychologists

BRITAIN
THE BRITISH PSYCHOLOGICAL SOCIETY
St Andrews House
48 Princess Road East
Leicester, LEI 7DR, UK
Tel: 0116 254 9568
E-mail: mail@bps.org.uk
Website: www.bps.org.ukHouse

Currently anyone can call themselves a psychologist in Britain. However, The Register of Chartered Psychologists was set up by The British Psychological Society to protect the public and help employers. If a member of the public consults or employs a Chartered Psychologist they can be assured that the person is properly trained, fully qualified, and answerable to an independent authority for professional actions.

Full registration

Full registration can be achieved through general application or through one of the accepted specialist groups within the register — Chartered Clinical Psychologist, Chartered Counselling Psychologist, Chartered Educational Psychologist, Chartered Forensic Psychologist, Chartered Health Psychologist, Chartered Occupational Psychologist.

General registration requires:

1. Passing a Qualifying Examination set by the Society;
   or
2. Obtaining a first degree conferred by a University or the Council for National Academic Awards for which psychology has been taken as a major subject and which is regarded by the Council as covering the general areas of psychology, at least as broadly as required by the Qualifying Examination referred to above, and to the same standard;
   or
3. For graduates not covered under either of the above, having such further experience or postgraduate qualification in psychology as shall assure the Council that the applicant has at least as broad a grasp of the general areas of psychology as that required by the Qualifying Examination referred to above and to the same standard; and
4. Since the date of passing the Qualifying Examination or equivalent studies mentioned above the applicant shall have successfully completed a period of study of, or practice in, psychology, or a combination of both, acceptable to the Council and shall be judged by the Council to have reached a standard sufficient for professional practice in psychology without supervision, the relevant period being of three years duration if full-time or an equivalent period of part-time or such greater period as the Council may stipulate.

Graduate basis for registration

Candidates for registration who have the qualifications referred to in either 1, 2 or 3 above may be referred to as having the 'Graduate Basis for Registration'.

UNITED STATES OF AMERICA

Registration

THE ASSOCIATION OF STATE AND PROVINCIAL PSYCHOLOGY
BOARDS (ASPPB)
P.O. Box 241245 | Montgomery, AL 36124-1245
E-mail: asppb@asppb.org
Website: www.asppb.org

In the United States (US) the registration board of each state controls licensing and registration. The Association of State and Provincial Psychology Boards (ASPPB) oversees and attempts to set unified standards in licensing for psychology boards across North America. It also allocates a licence, Certified Practising Qualification (CPQ), allowing psychologists to practise anywhere in North America (including Canada). To obtain a CPQ a psychologist must possess a current licence or registration to practise psychology at the independent level in an ASPPB member jurisdiction where such licence or registration is based on receipt of a doctoral degree in psychology; and have a record of practising psychology at the independent level for at least five years in an ASPPB member jurisdiction; and have no history of disciplinary actions (e.g., revocation, suspension, restriction) in any jurisdiction.

Professional membership

AMERICAN PSYCHOLOGICAL ASSOCIATION (APA)
750 First Street, NE, Washington, DC 20002-4242
E-mail: membership@apa.org
Website: www.apa.org

Full membership

To apply for the Member category, you must have a doctoral degree in psychology or a related field from a regionally accredited graduate or professional school or a school that achieved such accreditation within five years of the doctoral degree (or a school of similar standing outside of the US).This degree must be based, in part, upon a psychological dissertation or other evidence of proficiency in psychological scholarship.

Degrees from foreign institutions must show US equivalency. APA may require additional information to evaluate qualifications for membership.

Associate membership

To apply for the Associate Member category, you must have a Masters degree or have completed 2 years of graduate study in psychology or a related field at a regionally accredited institution. Degrees from foreign institutions must show US equivalency.

APA may require additional information to evaluate qualifications for membership.

AMERICAN PSYCHOLOGICAL SOCIETY (APS)
1010 Vermont Avenue, NW, Suite 1100
Washington, DC 20005-4907
Website: www.psychologicalscience.org

Membership
APS membership applicants must possess a doctoral degree in psychology (or related field) from an accredited institution or be able to show evidence of sustained contributions to scientific psychology.

Student affiliate
A range of affiliate memberships are available according to study level, for example, Graduate Student Affiliate, Undergraduate Student Affiliate.

CANADA

Registration
Registration requirements differ for each jurisdiction of Canada; however, it is a consistent requirement to have an approved (accredited) postgraduate qualification such as a Masters or Doctoral degree from an approved (accredited) psychology program, and to meet the regulated character requirements. Associate registration is normally available to psychologists under supervision. The CPQ is also available to more experienced psychologists through the ASPPB (see above).

Professional membership
CANADIAN PSYCHOLOGICAL ASSOCIATION (CPA)
141 Laurier Ave. West,
Suite 702
Ottawa, Ontario K1P 5J3
E-mail: cpamemb@cpa.ca
Website: www.cpa.ca

Full membership
Applicants for this category of membership must possess at least a Masters degree in psychology, or its academic equivalent, conferred by a graduate school of recognised standing.

Applicants must submit a completed application form providing all required information, also including the name of a Canadian Psychological Association (CPA) member who will sponsor your application. Sponsorship may be waived when a person is a member of another national/provincial or state psychological association, or who is a registered or certified psychologist in Canada, provided that the applicant meets all other requirements.

Student affiliates

Student Affiliates may be admitted into affiliation with the Association. Application for Student Affiliation, sponsored by a Fellow or Member of the Association, may be made at any time to the Head Office of the Association by graduate or undergraduate students (Honours or equivalent) in their upper years, who are enrolled and in full-time or part-time attendance at a recognised university and who are engaged in the study of psychology. Applications are to be reviewed in accordance with procedures to be established from time to time by resolution of the Board of Directors.

HONG KONG

Registration

The Registration Board of the Hong Kong Psychological Society was set up in May 1994. For registration a psychologist must:

- Be a member of the Society in good standing.
- Possess a higher degree in psychology obtained from an institution recognised by the Society; and
- Have at least one year of post-qualification experience in a discipline of psychology deemed acceptable by the Council.

Professional membership

THE HONG KONG PSYCHOLOGICAL SOCIETY LIMITED
Registered Address: The Department of Psychology,
The University of Hong Kong Pokfulam Road,
Hong Kong
E-mail: general_secretary@hkps.org.hk
Website: www.hkps.org.hk

Associate fellows

Must fulfil the requirements for graduate membership and, in addition, either possess a postgraduate qualification in psychology at Masters or Doctoral level and at least five years' working experience in the field (including the time required to obtain the postgraduate qualification) or at least six years' relevant working experience.

Graduate members

Must possess either an Honours degree for which psychology has been taken as a main subject, or a postgraduate qualification in psychology, from a university or other tertiary institution approved by the Council.

NEW ZEALAND

Registration

Registration as a psychologist in New Zealand is managed by the New Zealand Psychologists Board. The relevant legislation is the *Health Practitioners Competence Assurance Act 2003*. Registration may require a psychologist to undergo a period of supervision.

THE NEW ZEALAND PSYCHOLOGISTS BOARD
The Secretary
Psychologists Board
PO Box 10-140
Wellington
New Zealand
Fax: 64 4 472 2350
Tel: 64 4 499 7979
E-mail: bill.king@regboards.co.nz
Website: http://www.psychologistsboard.org.nz/

Full registration

The following qualifications are prescribed for registration as a psychologist in the general scope of practice:
- A minimum of a Masters degree in psychology from an accredited educational organisation, or an equivalent qualification, and
- a board-approved practicum or internship involving 1500 hours of supervised practice.

Trainee or intern psychologist

May be granted to applicants who:
- Have completed formal academic qualifications that have provided the trainee psychologist with the foundation competencies required for safe practice in the supervised setting, and
- Are entering board-approved supervised practice for the purpose of achieving full registration.

Professional membership

THE NEW ZEALAND PSYCHOLOGICAL SOCIETY
PO Box 4092
Wellington
E-mail: office@psychology.org.nz
Website: www.psychology.org.nz

Full membership

- Open to anyone who has a Doctorate, Masters or Honours degree in the field of psychology; an approved postgraduate degree in Education (at least two papers at that level will have been on psychological topics). In addition, either a thesis on a psychological topic

Becoming a Psychologist in Australia

must have been accepted or a minimum of one year's supervision acceptable to the Society has been undertaken;

- Equivalent qualifications or experience approved by the Society.

Subscribership
Subscribership is open to anyone who does not meet the criteria for full membership. Subscribers are entitled to receive all of the benefits of membership, including member rates on publications, preferential booking at conferences and advice from the society's office. Subscribers are not eligible to vote or hold office in the society.

Temporary subscribership is available for people who are residents overseas or newly arrived permanent residents in New Zealand who could qualify for full membership, but who cannot immediately obtain nomination for full membership as required under the rules. Temporary subscribership is available for a maximum period of up to one year after arrival in New Zealand.

BELGIUM
THE BELGIAN PSYCHOLOGICAL SOCIETY
Universiteit Ghent
Faculteit Psychologie en pedagogische wetenschappen
Henri Dunantlaan 2
B-9000 Gent, Belgium
Website: www.bvp-sbp.be

Full membership in the Belgian Psychological Society also makes you a member of the Belgian Federation of Psychology. This organisation was founded in 1979 and coordinates the existing associations of psychologists.

Full members
Must have a diploma of licentiate or doctor in the psychological sciences (1) delivered by a Belgian university or (2) delivered by a university from the European Union and recognised by the Belgian Commission of Psychologists.

Affiliate members
Are people whose main occupation is within the field of psychology and who fulfil one of the following conditions: (1) they reside in Belgium but do not hold a licentiate or doctoral degree in the psychological sciences, as requested of full members, or (2) they reside permanently outside Belgium.

EUROPE

EUROPEAN FEDERATION OF PSYCHOLOGISTS' ASSOCIATIONS (EFPA)
Website: www.efpa.be/Home/newpagina.htm

The European Federation of Psychologists' Associations (EFPA) is the leading Federation of National Psychology Associations. It provides a forum for European cooperation in a wide range of fields of academic training, psychology practice and research. There are 31 member associations of EFPA representing about 150,000 psychologists. The member organisations of EFPA are concerned with promoting and improving psychology as a profession and as a discipline, particularly, though not exclusively, in applied settings and with emphasis on the training and research associated with such practice.

In the context of EFPA, a psychologist is a person who has graduated in psychology from a university or equivalent institute of higher education, having undertaken a course in psychology recognised by their association, and who has fulfilled the criteria for professional status prescribed by that association.

In countries where there is legal recognition of psychologists, psychologists are those who are entitled, through registration, to call themselves psychologists and to practise professionally as such.

Recommended readings

Augoustinos, M., & Walker, I. (1995). *Social cognition*. London: Sage.

Banister, P., Burman, E., Parker, I., Taylor, M., & Tindall, C. (1994). *Qualitative methods in psychology: A research guide*. Buckingham, UK: Open University Press.

Benjamin, L. T. (1988). *A history of psychology: Original sources and contemporary research*. New York: McGraw-Hill.

Bickerton, D. (1995). *Language and human behavior*. Seattle, WA: University of Washington Press.

Breakwell, G. M., Hammond, S., & Fife-Shaw, C. (1995). *Research methods in psychology*. London: Sage.

Coleman, A. (2001). *Oxford dictionary of psychology*. New York: Oxford University Press.

Dennett, D. C. (1991). *Consciousness explained*. Boston: Brown.

DeVellis, R. F. (1991). *Scale development*. London: Sage

Eisner, E. W., & Peshkin, A. (1990). *Qualitative inquiry in education*. New York: Teachers College Press.

Fearn, N. (2001). *Zeno and the tortoise*. London: Atlantic.

Ferris, P. (1997). *Dr Freud: A life*. London: Random House.

Fisher, A., Sonn, C., & Bishop, B. J. (2002). *Psychological sense of community: Research, applications and implications*. New York: Plenum

Gayle, A., & Eysenck, M. W. (1992). *Handbook of individual differences: biological perspectives*. Chichester, UK: Wiley & Sons.

Grayling, A. C. (2003). *What is good?* London: Phoenix.

Gould, S. J. (1981). *The mismeasure of man*. London: Penguin

Hunt, M. (1993). *The story of psychology*. New York: Doubleday

Izard, C. E. (1991). *The psychology of emotions.* New York: Plenum Press.

Miller, G. (1966). *Psychology: The science of mental life.* Harmondsworth, UK: Pelican Books.

Mitchell, M., & Jolley, J. (1996). *Research design explained.* Orlando, FL: Harcourt Brace & Company.

Padgett, D. R. (2004). *The qualitative research experience.* Bellmont, CA: Wadsworth

Pickren, W. E., & Dewsbury A. (Eds.). *Evolving perspectives on the history of psychology.* Washington, DC: APA.

Pinker, S. (1997). *How the mind works.* London: Penguin.

Sternberg, R. J. (1982). *The handbook of human intelligence.* New York: Cambridge University Press.

Super, C. M., & Super, D. E. (2001). *Opportunities in psychology careers.* Chicago, IL: McGraw Hill.

White, B. (1993). *The first three years of life.* New York: Simon & Schuster.

Becoming a Psychologist in Australia

References

American Psychological Association. (2006). *About APA*. Retrieved June 23, 2006, from htpp://www.apa.org/about

Australian Psychological Society. (2006). *About the APS*. Retrieved June 23, 2006, from http://www.psychology.org.au/aps/default.asp

The Macquarie dictionary (3rd ed.). (1997). Sydney, Australia: Macquarie University.

Psychologists Registration Act 2000 (Victoria) (2001). *Psychologists Registration Act 2000*. Victorian Government Act No 41/2000. Retrieved June 23, 2006, from http://www.dms.dpc.vic.gov.au/

www.ingramcontent.com/pod-product-compliance
Lightning Source LLC
Chambersburg PA
CBHW070931270326
41927CB00011B/2810